RETAIL SPACES

small stores

under 250 m² [2,700 sq. ft.]

RETAIL SPACES

small stores

under 250 m² [2,700 sq. ft.]

Judy Shepard
and the editors of *Retail Design International*

RSD Publishing, Inc. New York, NY

RSD Publishing, Inc.
302 Fifth Avenue
New York, NY 10001
212-279-7004
CS@rsdpublishing.com
www.rsdpublishing.com

Distributors to the trade in the United States and Canada
Innovative Logistics
575 Prospect Street
Lakewood NJ 08701
732-363-5679

Distributors outside the United States and Canada
HarperCollins International
10 East 53rd Street
New York, NY 10022-5299

Library of Congress Cataloging in Publication Data:
Retail Spaces: Small Stores under 250 m2 (2,700 sq. ft.)

Printed and Bound in Hong Kong
ISBN: 978-0-9826128-2-8

CONTENTS

How much can a designer do with a small or even tiny space? And, can a retailer truly brand its store and allow products to shine in a space that others might write off as too cramped, confined, restricted or just hopelessly small?

On these pages you'll see evidence that the answer to the above questions are: *a great deal,* and an emphatic *yes.* The retail spaces shown here prove that not only is it possible for a small store to be effective, but the creatively teamed retailer and designer can actually rise above much larger competition and turn a space limitation into an advantage.

Budget constraints are of course, the very reason why many of these stores are small, and it's not surprising that many of the designers struggle with having to do a lot with very little. But, manage they do, using the most effective weapon in their arsenal — creativity. They utilize valuable resources where most needed, or most noticeable, and source inexpensive materials elsewhere. They use color and light and ingenuity to create environments that support the brand, be it elegant and upscale, fun and exciting, or young and hip.

TARGET MARKET

Perhaps the most vital component to the success of these small retailers is *know thy customer.* Again and again designers featured here talk about catering to target markets. The successful small retailer has no room to waste on trying to please everyone, or even almost everyone. They clearly define their audience first, and then figure how, and with what, to appeal to those specific people.

Once that all-important target is defined the smaller retailer is at an advantage; everything within the customer's sight — and the entire store is often within the customer's sight — is desirable. The results are a focused environment in which a target customer finds exactly what they want without an exhaustive search — translating to sales and customer loyalty.

What store could be more focused than London Foot Patrol? This retailer knows exactly who will walk into the door, and exactly what they will buy. The designers simply developed a concept to match their demographic. The owners of Judith & Charles in Toronto have thought long and hard about the women who shop their store and select both products and design elements to match. A different market and a different product, Vespa in Mexico, results in a completely different store.

FLEXIBILITY

Another element you'll find in most of these small stores is flexibility. Fixtures and shelving can be rearranged and adjusted and visual merchandising can be continually updated to hold interest and repeat business.

Clarkes Jewelers in Shreveport, Louisiana needed a design that would allow the owners to move the display units — and the lighting overhead — as product demand fluctuates. At Jaeger London, the timber-framed fixtures that appear casually propped against the wall are both form and function.

VARIETY

In this collection of successful small stores it's encouraging to see the variety within the variety. It's not surprising to see certain product categories well represented in a book on small stores. However, it is surprising or perhaps just heartwarming, to see the great diversity within those categories. Optical stores range from the laid-back California beach vibe of Malibu's 9026 Eyes (also the smallest store in this book), to the sleek modern design of Gaston Optik in the Czech Republic, and on to the elegant charm of Lakeland Optical in Jackson, Mississippi.

There is also ample proof on these pages that telecom stores need not blend endlessly into one another: See the vibrant pink of 4010 in Cologne; the immersive environment of COX Communications in Louisiana; and the open, inviting atmosphere of Nextel in Santiago. Even within one brand, PUMA, a store in Paris and another in New York City look nothing alike.

IN-MALL

Also represented here are a large number of in-mall stores. When shoppers have so much choice literally at hand, these retailers face the unique challenge of standing out amongst a surrounding clutter of popcorn kiosks, sulky teenagers and squealing two-year-olds. These stores must signal to members of their target audience, to "look this way."

In-mall Verona Vibe gets noticed with the color red; Intermezzo with dynamic lines and shapes, Crusoe with dramatic lighting and eye-catching graphics and Brida Shoes with a strong color scheme and hard-to-miss presence.

First up is a truly small, 35 m2 optical store in beautiful Malibu. Then it's off to Madrid for some fine jewelry before heading to Santiago for a pair of shoes. Enjoy the trip.

9026 Eyes

Malibu, California

MASHstudios
Los Angeles

9025 Eyes is a luxury eyewear store located in the super-chic Malibu Country Mart, and designed by MASHstudios of Los Angles. The store, named after the location's prestigious 90265 zip code, supplies sunglasses — that all-important beach-life accessory — to who's who in Malibu.

MASHstudios first worked with the retailer in

their store in Westlake Village where the designers installed sleek, black elements and floating cases ideal for showcasing products in a city setting. With 9026 Eyes' return to its former seaside home in Malibu, the owners called upon MASHstudios to develop a more relaxed space.

The new Malibu store is drenched in vintage

beach charm. The environment feels sunny and welcoming without having completely abandoned the steamlined, modern persona that MASHstudios had established in the Westlake Village location.

Built-in display cases feature integrated backlighting that eliminates shadows and surrounds the eyewear with a gorgeous glow. Solid teak driftwood-like drawers line the white walls, adding a distressed, airy aesthetic to the clean lines and angles. Cabinets and furniture are all scaled down to keep the store open, but every square inch of space is calculated and fully utilized.

"Working with such a tiny space was one of our greatest challenges," states Bernard Brucha of MASHstudios. *"We needed to present quite a few eyeglasses, but didn't want the product to appear cramped or disorganized. Our solution was to eliminate excess visual noise like external hardware on the cabinets. Everything was reduced to the bare minimum. We chose to use solid wood to complement the rustic feel of the country market without being 'country kitchen'.*

"Mid-century-inspired, fold-out bobby-legged tables and eclectic seating help conjure the era of transistor radios and a sense of California dreamin'," continues Brucha. *"The medium-toned wood and the hair-pin table legs give this new space a throwback vibe while simultaneously preserving the sophistication of 9026 Eyes' high-end optics."*

ABOVE: Integrated backlighting eliminates shadows and surrounds the eyewear with a gorgeous glow. **BELOW:** The designers eliminated excess visual noise like external hardware on the cabinets.

Mid-century-inspired, fold-out bobby-legged tables and eclectic seating help conjure the era of transistor radios and a sense of California dreamin'.

DESIGN
MASHstudios, Los Angeles, CA

STORE SIZE
28 m2 (300 sq. ft.)

CUSTOM MILLWORK / CUSTOM LIGHTING
MASHstudios, Los Angeles, CA

PHOTOGRAPHY
Haris Sarantis

OhmyGOd
Madrid

MARKETING-JAZZ
Madrid

The branding of this tiny jewelry store in Madrid started with an idea and a store name. The idea was to open a jewelry store that would become a trend-setter in the wider world of fashion, and the store name, OhmyGOd, was simply the phrase, "oh my God" that customers would exclaim upon seeing the space and the stunning jewelry on display. In other words — the wow factor.

Both the idea and the name were put to designer Carlos Aires of MARKETING-JAZZ by Cinthya Nicolás, project developer and third generation jeweler. Aires and the Nicolás family worked together, and the extraordinary results are shown here.

From the start of the project everyone understood that to create a trend-setting shop, attention must be paid not only to the design of the space, but also to supply and demand — the merchandise had to be fabulous and the customers had to be treated like royalty when they were in the store.

The concept behind the store name was used as a guide when making design and product-purchasing decisions: If the first impression was "oh my God" then the choice was considered sound.

One of the first decisions concerned the shop window. It had to be large and open, taking the shop out onto the street and allowing the space to be seen in its entirety from the sidewalk. Other key elements in the design were the striking, custom-designed floor covering and the bright color of the walls. Both had to not only get attention from the street but also become associated in customers' minds with the store brand.

Display cases on the right- and left-hand walls differ from each other in style and the sort of items they display. On the left-hand wall, modern display cases display the newest items, while the ornate in-set cases on the right hold the most valuable pieces.

Presiding over the cash/wrap and adding her personality to the space is a large picture of Patricia Nicolás, the store's creative director.

OPPOSITE PAGE: The entire space can be taken in at a glance. A custom lighting fixture above the central display reminds customers as to where they are. **TOP LEFT:** The front window allows passersby a clear view of the store and showcases. In addition to jewelry, fashion magazines that feature items for sale in the store are on display. **ABOVE RIGHT:** The central display area consists of display tables of different heights. **ABOVE LEFT:** Ornate frames give the inset display cases on the right-hand wall the look of old-master paintings. These cases hold the most valuable items.

DESIGN
MARKETING-JAZZ, Madrid

STORE SIZE
34 m2 (366 sq. ft.)

CREATIVE DIRECTOR AND FURNITURE DESIGN
Carlos Aires

ILLUSTRATIONS AND SKETCHES
Elena de Andrés

PHOTOGRAPHY
Luis Sanchez de Pedro Aires

Guante

Mall Plaza Alameda, Santiago

dearQ Architecture & Design
Santiago

For Guante, a men's shoes and accessories chain that has been a trendsetter for more than 80 years, their newest shop in the Mall Plaza Alameda, is a triumph of design over space — or the lack of space. The store, designed by dearQ Architecture & Design, is only about 37 m2. Storage is on an upper level and the lower lever, shown here, is used only for presentation and selling.

The neutral black/gray and white color scheme is introduced on the shop front with its black clad façade and raised window in which the shoes are showcased as if they were works of art. Inside, the perimeter side walls are lined with illuminated, glass shelves contained within slick, shiny black frames. Featured merchandise get special treatment on the white-topped fixtures in the center of the shop that also serve as seating for shoppers trying on the shoes.

Toward the rear of the space, under a reflective black canopy filled with MR16 lamps and a shiny black back wall that carries the logo/name, is the simple, cube-like cash/wrap desk. To one side of it, in recessed gray cabinets outlined in white are some of the leather accessories carried in the store. A full-length mirror, opposite, completes the layout. The black tinted wood floor and the glistening, reflective black surfaces "give the store a touch of elegance," said Marcela Ponce de Leon Salucci, the Principal in Charge of the design team.

DESIGN
dearQ Architecture & Design, Santiago, Chile

STORE SIZE
37 m2 (400 sq. ft.)

PRINCIPAL IN CHARGE
Marcela Ponce de Leon Salucci

PHOTOGRAPHY
Courtesy of dearQ Architecture & Design

Foot Patrol

Concept Store, Berwick Street, London

Brinkworth/Wilson Brothers
London

The new Foot Patrol shop on Berwick Street in London is as unique as the one-off, one-of-a-kind sneakers that it sells. Designed as a collaboration between Brinkworth and Wilson Brothers, both of London, Foot Patrol is a shop-within-a-shop.

From the sidewalk the "first" façade is understated and unassuming, and gives little hint to what will greet the customer once inside the door. A "second" shop, complete with its own façade, has been constructed to "float" within the outer store shell.

The narrow inner shop has been assembled from recycled scaffold planks for the floor, walls and pitched roof. Fixtures of satin black steel complete the urban look of the tiny shop. A full mirror on the end wall creates an optical illusion that makes the store appear to extend infinitely.

Lighting systems and services are concealed behind the pitched roof of the inner shop, allowing room for a sliding library-style display system that can be extended the entire length of the store or nested at either end to leave space for special events or promotions.

Murray Aitken of Brinkworth concludes, *"This blend of modularity and function, offset with an aged vintage backdrop, creates the perfect stage for the final detail. The original, revered Foot Patrol gas mask logo, housed within an aged metal frame and rendered in white neon, meets customers as they enter the store through the 'transition' space, the antechamber where the outer and inner stores meet."*

TOP: The outer facade. **ABOVE:** The original Foot Patrol gas mask logo greets customers on the "inner" facade.

DESIGN
Brinkworth, London
Wilson Brothers, London

STORE SIZE
50 m2 (538 sq. ft.)

DESIGNERS
**Ben Wilson, Oscar Wilson,
Adam Brinkworth, Murray Aitken**

PHOTOGRAPHER
Louise Melchior

ABOVE: The long, narrow space of the "floating" inner shop celebrates rather than disguises the small size of the store.
BELOW: Steel fixtures can be retracted to make room for parties — an important component at Foot Patrol, London's premier destination sneaker store.

Evita, Espacio Urbano La Dehesa

Santiago, Chile

Droguett A&A Ltda

Santiago, Chile

Elegance, but not in the classic way, style that pushes the borders of the definition, is the design concept chosen for the Evita, Espacio Urbano La Dehesa shop, the chain's fifth store, located at Lo Barnechea in Santiago, Chile. Freddy Droguett of the design firm Droguett A&A Ltda, describes the identity of the newest store as, "Transgressive Elegance. It's elegance for a woman of these times, one who is self-confident and not attached to the dogmas of fashion. The goal of the store design was to achieve an environment that was both formal and informal to capture the middle and high income sophisticated 18 to 35-year-old woman who embodies that refinement."

The Evita boutique specializes in upscale clothing for special events such as weddings, cocktail and graduation parties. As such, the old classic ballroom look was the base concept. The entire style and design, the bricks, huge replica doors, store fixtures, and flooring were inspired by the Chilean colonial period.

Upon entering, customers are enveloped by the store's atmosphere that has been made to look like a dignified forgotten ballroom restored to some of its old glory. Finely detailed cabinetry is strategically placed throughout the store. The striking exterior and interior were constructed to resemble old walls crumbling after years of neglect leaving only the Chilean clay bricks exposed with squeezed out mortar. Eye-pleasing turquoise paint bathes the interior surfaces, creating a peaceful background, while baseboard cove up-lighting amplifies the effect and turns the walls into giant pieces of heavily textured art. Backlit pictures and showcases seem to

Mahogany flooring was given a vintage appearance by filling each board's distressed joint edge with black paste.

TOP: Baseboard cove uplighting highlights the wall texture. **ABOVE LEFT:** Display window from outside the mall. **ABOVE RIGHT:** Store entrance from the Mall. The neutral outside color was chosen to contrast vividly with the turqoise interior.

LEFT: Three doors, used to exhibit accessories, back the cashier counter and the outside show window. **BELOW LEFT:** Inside the store looking out to the mall interior.

DESIGN
Droguett A&A ltda, Santiago, Chile

STORE SIZE
70 m2 (750 sq. ft.)

ARCHITECT, DIRECTOR
Freddy Droguett H.

ARCHITECT, PROJECT DESIGNER
María Antonieta Cepeda

GENERAL CONTRACTOR
Andres Link, Constructora LNK

STORE CEO
Alex Cattan

PRODUCT MANAGER
Evelyn Alamo

PHOTOGRAPHER
Marcos Mendizábal

A rich, dark-on-dark wallpaper covers the fitting room walls, while two large red doors used as scarf displays frame the entrance.

float free of their surroundings, further enhancing the textured look of the ostensibly crumbling walls.

Rich antique-colored floors of distressed mahogany, laid diagonally in geometric patterns, separate different areas of the store. In an alcove tucked on one side, the fitting room walls in highly contrasting dark wallpaper provide a distinct separation from the store itself. Two huge red lacquer-painted doors, used as scarf displays, form the fitting rooms' entryway. The sophisticated deep red is repeated in the cash wrap/cashier cabinetry and an imposing tall garment/accessories display unit on the other side. As though they didn't want to remove antique moldings, the coffered ceiling effect was created to further the historic homage to the theme of old ballrooms. A tasteful chandelier with a mix of traditional and modern flair hangs from one of them, while PAR 30 spotlights surrounding the

ceiling perimeter beautifully highlight and isolate the clothing displays and heighten the charm of the store.

Unlike most metal frames of exterior store windows, which are left as the mall or building installed them, this store's window framing has been given a faux paint treatment to simulate old rusted iron. Huge paneled doors made in the antique colonial period style are used as backgrounds for the window displays, and cashier cabinetry on their reverse side, to present an image of upper class and grand distinction of a bygone era.

This elegant 70m2 store delivers a spacious ambiance for customers as they shop the spotlighted displays of upscale clothing and accessories.

Hush Puppies Kids
Antofagasta, Concepcion, Santiago

dearQ Architecture & Design
Santiago

In a relatively small space — less than 750 sq. ft. — Marcela Ponce de Leon Salucci, principal of dearQ Architecture & Design created a world for children's shoes. This new Hush Puppies Kids shop, in the Concepcion district of Santiago, has created a new look and life for the long-established brand.

As Ponce de Leon Salucci describes it, the shop is *"a world based on curves, soft and flowing shapes where color and imagination are always present. The idea was to give children an environment where they feel they are a part of it, and the dog (the Hush Puppies icon) is their own pet."*

The arched entrance of the façade introduces the tunnel-like theme found inside the store. The signature red curved overhead panel, that starts at the door and leads to the rear of the space, tends to lower the ceiling and scales the space to a child's eye level. The tunnel also creates a fantasy world with colorful graphics. The icon basset hound, in a focal red circular frame, brings the whole shop into focus. The red circle becomes the dog house for everybody's favorite puppy. The same circular motif appears on the façade where a series of circles, next to the entrance, act as bulls-eye shadow boxes for featured shoes. The motif reappears again inside the store on the wall behind the soft, curved, red-plastic cash/wrap. The signature red color also appears on the pouf seats that are scaled to a child's size for trying on the shoes.

White acrylic is the material of choice for most of the store's wall and floor fixtures. The material often appears with soft, rounded forms and according to Ponce de Leon Salucci, *"It gives the store a light* *sensation and at the same time gives the products all color protagonism."* To keep the children amused while parents are occupied perusing the available stock, there is an interactive video game available for the kids to play where — naturally — the main character is the Hush Puppies puppy.

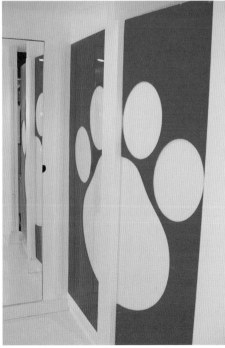

DESIGN
dearQ Architecture & Design, Santiago, Chile

STORE SIZE
70 m2 (750 sq. ft.)

PRINCIPAL IN CHARGE
Marcela Ponce de Leon Salucci

PHOTOGRAPHY
dearQ Architecture & Design

Magic Attic

Derby, United Kingdom

Dalziel and Pow Design Consultants

London

DESIGN
Dalziel and Pow Design Consultants, London, UK

STORE SIZE
70 m2 (750 sq. ft.)

PHOTOGRAPHY
Dalziel and Pow Design Consultants

Magic Attic, so named by Dalziel and Pow Design Consultants, is an off-shoot of the Save The Children organization. The concept was to raise the profile of Save The Children, showcase their work, and connect more closely with local mothers and children in a welcoming retail environment.

The 70 m2 space was refitted to include new and recycled products for children and pregnant women. In addition to books, toys, clothing and equipment, there is a selection of healthy drinks for sale as well as fair trade coffee and home made snacks. An important area in the shop is the activity zone where children can play, be kept amused and occupied while also raising awareness of some of the vital work going on worldwide by Save The Children.

As is to be expected, Dalziel and Pow was also challenged by a very low budget. To quote the designers: *"We decided to create a dramatic focal point in the scheme with a strong architectural form anchoring the cash desk and promotional stock, finished in bright orange Marmoleum."*

The rest of the scheme relied heavily on bright, strong colors and amusing graphics. Working within set guidelines, custom graphics were designed to suit the brief *"to delight children."* There is a game set out on the floor — somewhat like Snakes and Ladders, but designed to emphasize Save The Children issues — a fun height chart and a magnetic map of the world. The latter can be used to show artwork done by children in the store.

Featured in the store's window is a Yak gondola: a life size, cut-out yak that not only displays merchandise, but also holds topical graphics. The yak is also a reminder that for a donation of 160 pounds (about $255) a real yak can be provided to a family who will gather its wool, its milk and also get a hearty assist from the animal when it comes to ploughing the fields.

Dalziel and Pow undertook this assignment on a "not for profit" basis, operating at cost, and the suppliers who were involved in producing this shop either contributed materials at cost or at heavily discounted prices. With the assist of suppliers such as I Guzzini (lighting), Stylo Graphics (environmental graphics) and MZK (merchandising systems, midfloor gondolas and the yak), the store was fitted on budget, and in just three weeks. As Dalziel and Pow says, considering it was a new concept and included a new accessible toilet and baby changing area, *"Not bad!"*

Espoir
Seoul

JHP Design Consultancy
London

JHP, a London-based design consultancy, enjoyed responding to the challenge set to them by Espoir — a new cosmetic brand. Espoir's challenge was for JHP not only to create all aspects of the architecture and store design, but to position the brand, create the brand identity, design the staff uniforms, and oversee the launch campaign. In addition to all that, Espoir would be competing with brands like M.A.C. and Bobbi Brown. The appeal therefore had to be global — to appeal *"to fashionable young women across the world."*

The circular platforms out front and the sweeping curve of the corner window, plus the flush of the rich but subtle orange color, set the Espoir shop apart from the surrounding retail stores and also steps forward with a strong feminine appeal. That orange color, plus purple, appear as the brand's signature colors. According to the JHP design team, *"We selected these colors to reflect the contemporary nature of our fashionista client, to express the brand's values and to transport it to the world of what luxury brands do so well — which is creating eye-catching, directional and iconic brand statements."*

The interior is basically a "raw shell" furnished with "slick furniture items" and "stylist closet-inspired fixtures." Added to this are polished plaster, concrete, antique glass and leather. Purple crystal chandeliers hang above the white floor and the white fixtures with purple accents and smoky gray Lucite. An unusual three-part hinged folding cabinet/ screen — in purple and white — and self-illuminated, serves as a "stylist closet" on the floor. Focal walls and a large plexi panel with the store name emblazoned on it are all in the signature orange color and they bounce forward into the otherwise white walled space.

According to the designers, *"Espoir has the most authoritative range of make-up in the marketplace. From the outset, the standards were set as high as possible. We and Espoir worked closely with top stylists and make-up artists"* to assure that the results would be right. TV series *Gossip Girl* lead actress/model, Leighton Meester is the "face" of the brand and her image appears in photos taken by the legendary Hollywood photographer Mark Liddel.

TOP: Fixtures are inspired by the equipment used by professional stylists. An unusual three-part hinged folding cabinet/screen — in purple and white and self-illuminated — serves as a "stylist closet" on the floor.

DESIGN
JHP Design Consultancy, London, UK

STORE SIZE
79 m2 (850 sq. ft.)

congstar
Cologne, Germany

Dula
Dortmund, Germany

congstar's bright colors and bold graphics are designed to appeal to its youthful market.

congstar, a subsidiary of Deutsche Telekom AG, offers its customers nationwide affordable mobile service and internet phone, broadband internet access and, until recently, was sold only online or through its sales partners. Now, in cooperation with the Telekom Shop, the brand provides a live experience for its customers with its own store. The first shop to open, shown here, is located in Cologne — "at home" so to speak, in the same city in which congstar is headquartered.

As Mr. Martin Knauer, the managing director of congstar points out, the question of location was of immense importance — it was kind of a must to locate the store in Cologne as the congstar HQ is also located in Cologne. A special motto for the congstar store was created: 'Let's congstarize Cologne!' congstar is the first discounter for telecommunication products with its own store in which a complete range of products is offered.

The company's target market is derived from its discount price structure and includes young people looking for affordability and flexible options — a customer perhaps not inclined to approach the "traditional" telecom stores. The look and style of the congstar brand — both online and in-store — is designed to appeal to this young market.

Bright colors — yellow, orange, blue and green in bold graphic shapes — pop out from black backgrounds and dark gray floors. Even the façade features this invigorating mix of color and design.

Signage is anything but static as it suspends from the ceiling and juts out from feature walls. Adding strength to the already bright colors and focusing attention onto the signage and merchandise are overhead lights, also in bright colors.

In keeping with the importance young people often place on social causes and community, congstar combines its low prices with a high degree of social commitment. Proceeds from the sale of the branded T-shirts, sweaters and bags, available only at the store, go to an organization, Baskets for Cologne, that helps young people living in poverty. The organization offers sports and a range of events including career counseling. In addition, customers can try their luck at Nintendo basketball — for every ten virtual baskets made, one euro goes to the charitable organization.

Proceeds from the sale of congstar's branded merchandise goes to a local charity.

DESIGN/SHOPFITTING
Dula, Dortmund, Germany

STORE SIZE
80 m2 (861 sq. ft.)

PHOTOGRAPHY
Dula

The small space packs a big punch with color, lighting, dynamic fixture design and signage that emphasizes affordablility.

Key West

Sainte-Catherine Street, Montréal

GHA design studios

TOP LEFT: The illuminated walls produce a glowing jewel box effect that beckon to passersby. **TOP RIGHT:** The cash counter uses Lumi-Sheet® to digitally display the Key West name. **ABOVE:** Dashes of red racing stripes on the floor draw customers towards the rear of the store.

The white drywall ceiling appears to float against the painted black ceiling and the black top wall tier. Hidden in plain sight, the black ventilation duct was relocated to the middle of the ceiling to become an important design element.

Key West, a seller of brand-name sunglasses and sport watches, wanted to open a new store with a clear and cohesive design concept — something missing in its other locations. To this end the retailer hired GHA design studios to design a new store in a former souvenir shop on busy, touristy, Saint Catherine Street in Montréal.

Debbie Kalisky, Director of Retail Development explains, "The objective with this high visibility location in the heart of Montréal's downtown action was to create a flagship statement for the company and solidify its role as the sunglass and sports watch authority."

Only the top name brands from each category are sold at this location and the emphasis is on brand identification and recognition. Within the shop each designer has a designated display unit with their name applied in bold black letters on a glass panel.

The small size of the space — only 900 sq. ft. — proved to be challenging. In order to create as much physical space as possible in the narrow store, the ceiling height was raised to the structural deck and extensive architectural intervention opened up the entrance.

Kalisky says, "The 'bowling alley' configuration of

the store was dealt with by concentrating the merchandise along the walls and having only two narrow illuminated display cases in the center. The cash counter was relegated to the very rear of the store in order to avoid a bottleneck in the middle."

A layering effect along the store perimeter is achieved through creative use of transparency and luminescence. All merchandising units, whether vertical or horizontal, have backlit Lumi-Sheet® with integrated LED lighting to offset the product offering — dark sunglasses and watches appear to float on the illuminated surfaces. A new logo developed for Key West is applied as "wallpaper" above the display units and behind the cash wrap. Transparent glass panels offset from the wallpaper with stainless steel spacers add depth. On the facade, the logo wallpaper is applied as a film to the inside of the glass.

As a pioneer in the self-service model of high-end sunglasses, not a single pair of sunglasses is kept behind glass. A magnetic tag sets off a sophisticated alarm system if the product approaches the front door. The danger of shrinkage (surprising low given the location), is far outweighed by the advantage to Key West of being in an area of such high visibility.

DESIGN
GHA design studios

STORE SIZE
84 m2 (900 sq. ft.)

LIGHTING
Juno

GENERAL CONTRACTOR AND FIXTURES
Couvrette Construction

GRAPHICS
Media Graf

PHOTOGRAPHER
Yves Lefebvre, Montréal

Levi's Icon Store "Buttenheim"

Berlin

Plajer & Franz Studio

Berlin

Levi's Icon Store "Buttenheim" is a small concept store in Berlin that was recently redesigned by Plajer & Franz Studio. The two primary challenges for the designers were the tight schedule — the store had to be completed in just five weeks in order to be open for Berlin's fashion week — and an equally tight budget.

The vision for the redesign was to create a space with the ambiance of an old, loft-style apartment, with a hint of industrial charm mixed in.

The 87 m2 space is divided into two rooms, separated by two steps. To connect these rooms the designers placed a large, wooden display table directly over the stairs. Accompanied by — and on one end supported by — old, cast-iron radiators, this stair-straddling table creates an important transition point between the rooms and allows one central display to serve the entire store — effectively turning the two rooms into one cohesive whole.

Throughout the store vintage window frames — of various sizes and styles — are utilized as display fixtures and support both shelving and hang rods. While some of the windows' original glass panes are still in place, others have been replaced with acrylic panes with "places-to-be" in Berlin printed on them. In addition to holding featured merchandise, items reflecting the brand's American West heritage, such as a cow skull, are interspersed.

Adding to the rustic look of the store are pieces from old doors — in their original, paint-chipped state — that form both the fitting room doors and the cash/wrap counter.

The finished store, with its vintage elements and Levi's iconic merchandise, artfully combines Berlin culture and the famous brand.

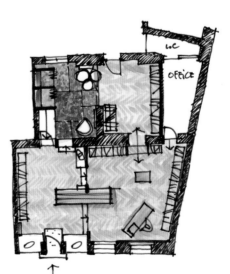

ABOVE: A "Monteray" sign pays homage to the brand's early days in the San Francisco area. **LEFT:** Meanwhile, the German birthplace of founder Levi Strauss, Buttenheim, appears on the facade.

THIS PAGE AND OPPOSITE BOTTOM: Old window casings serve as display fixtures throughout the store. Shelves and hang rods are interspersed with Western props and some of the window panes enclose clear acrylic printed with Berlin's "places-to-be."

DESIGN
Plajer & Franz Studio, Berlin, Germany

STORE SIZES
87 m2 (936 sq. ft.)

PROJECT MANAGEMENT
Jochen Buder

PHOTOGRAPHER
Ken Schluchtmann, diephotodesigner.de

Vintage doors, luggage and rugs appear in the fitting rooms, all contributing to the overall rustic look of the store.

3 Mobil

Bruuns Gallery, Aarhus, Denmark

Riis Retail

Kolding, Denmark

ABOVE: A huge "3" greets customers at the door. **LEFT:** A well-lit counter allows productive customer/ representative communication.

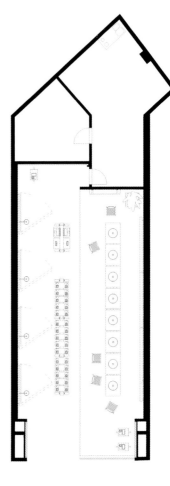

Designed by Riis Retail, this 3 Mobil shop recently opened in the Bruuns Gallery shopping center located in the center of Aarhus, Denmark. 3 Mobil is part of the "3" brand of mobile communications headquartered in Hong Kong and operating in Denmark, Australia, Austria, Indonesia, Republic of Ireland, Italy, Sweden, Macau and United Kingdom.

The concept behind this space was to combine a "selling shop" and a "lifestyle shop" into one cohesive unit. To achieve this in such a small space required the complete fusion of function and form. Every aspect of

DESIGN
Riis Retail A/S, Kolding, Denmark
Dennis Madsen, Jacob Guldmann

STORE SIZE
90 m2 (969 sq. ft.)

TECHNICAL ASSISTANT
Gitte Barsøe Hansen

PRODUCT DEVELOPMENT
Torben Vad Nissen

PRODUCT MANAGER
Niels Kjær

PHOTOGRAPHER
Jens Peter Engedal

TOP AND ABOVE: The 90 m2 space can be seen in a glance and navigated with ease.

TOP LEFT: The open arms of a large lifestyle photo invite customers to try out the goods. **TOP RIGHT:** Products displays are "draped" over a center beam. **ABOVE RIGHT AND LEFT:** Branding is everywhere; the signature "3" appears on the end of the beam and even on a planter.

ABOVE LEFT: The oak flooring continues behind the counters. **ABOVE RIGHT:** Wall-filling signage reinforces the "3" brand and explains the products and services.

the design — every element and detail — had to communicate its purpose and instantly convey the "3" brand to the consumer.

The store layout is extremely straightforward and enables customers to orient themselves instantly upon entering. In the center of the store products are "draped" over a round wooden beam running from the entrance to the back of the store. Large signage on the left-hand wall communicate the "3" universe, while counters to the right allow private interaction between client and representative.

Brand identity can be seen throughout the space. A huge "3" greets customers on the facade and then

repeats itself inside on the wall and on signage. Large lifestyle photos of inviting and friendly models are placed behind key product displays.

The color palette is limited and controlled by the materials used — oak wood, white Corian and white steel — and helps to simplify and brand the space. The light-colored oak appears not only on the floor, but also on a wall and the sides of the counters. The oak adds warmth to the space as it reflects onto the surrounding white surfaces — walls, counter tops and signage. Accents of blue complete the palette and keep the look clean, simple and welcoming.

Gaston Optik

Brno, Czech Republic

Fandament Architects/Hast Retail sro

Brno/Ostrava, Czech Republic

Gaston Optik has been a leading optometrists in Brno for many years, selling contact lenses and designer frames from Alain Mikli, Philippe Starck, Blac, Ludwig Rosenberger and many others. Hast Retail sro and Fandament sro were recently charged with the design of the retailer's 90 m2, in-mall space.

Of central importance to the design is the concept of space — the effective use and division of the limited number of available square meters. For the average customer it's, at first glance, merely an attractive place to try on and choose a pair of glasses; however, for the professional optometrists and sales staff the finished store is a carefully interconnected mosaic of zones or departments designed to create sufficient space and privacy for the various needs of the retailer.

A row of three white counters, or "islands" are placed at regular intervals to one side of the space, serving various functions such as presentation and cash/wrap. These counters lead to the small, gold-lined "box" or " golden nugget" where eye examinations are given and contact lens are fitted. This small space, distinct from the rest of the interior,

sits next to the entrance and creates a tiny shop-within-shop effect.

The clean, white, minimal design of the space, with its sleek lines and reflective surfaces, focuses all attention onto the merchandise. Each frame is carefully placed to showcase its uniqueness and desirability. A grid pattern of display cases adds to the modernist atmosphere while comfortable chairs in bright green serve as playful accents points. Overall lighting is warm and soft except for blue highlights focused on the products themselves.

The gold lining of the optometrists "shop-within-a-shop" reinforces the jewelry box visual presentation of the entire shop.

Display fixtures hanging in front of the windows allow the products to be seen from inside and out, and give a sense of increased floor space.

DESIGN
Fandament Architects/Hast Retail sro
Brno/Ostrava, Czech Republic

STORE SIZE
90 m2 (969 sq. ft.)

The designers envisioned the shop as a "jewelry box" in which the frames are showcased like pieces of fine jewelry. The overall white palette allows the accents of green and gold to stand out, and blue lighting on the frames themselves contrasts with the overall soft, warm lighting.

Brida Shoes

White Oaks Mall, London, Ontario

GHA design studios

ABOVE LEFT: The wide, open storefront emphasizes the notion of affordable fashion and accessibility. This openness contrasts with the mysterious smoky glass and black mosaic of the show window that invites customers to come close and discover what goodies might be inside. **TOP:** The feature display fixture in the center of the store is completely modular and re-configured according to season. **ABOVE RIGHT:** Luxurious materials are used sparingly in the project and reserved for the back and sides of the storefront display window

Given the small space, it was quite a feat to designate a cash area with its own personality. The solution was to nestle the customer within an all-encompassing black and red floral experience.

DESIGN
GHA design studios

STORE SIZE
93 m2 (1,000 sq. ft.)

GENERAL CONTRACTOR
Entasis Inc.
Project Design Management

MILLWORK
Maple Leaf Millwork

SIGN
Roland's Neon Signs

GRAPHICS
Signature Graphics

FLOORING
FloorMart

LIGHTING
The Lighting Boutique &
Appliance Shoppe

PHOTOGRAPHER
Philip Castleton

Brida, a family-owned import/export and wholesale shoe business founded in Venezuela in 1985, recently relocated a portion of its retail sector to Ontario to focus on selling fashion-forward shoes at affordable prices. The owners asked GHA design studios to create a retail outlet that would transform Brida into a high-fashion brand while remaining accessible and non-exclusive.

The product line in this White Oaks Mall store, unlike other Brida locations, is streamlined to carry only women's footwear. The target customer is a fashion-conscious woman who is highly influenced by trends, yet still value-driven. The dominant store colors of black and red are meant to speak to this strong, confident woman.

The results had to be distinctively feminine to reflect the product offering, yet make a strong visual statement. *"The goal was to design a space with maximum visual impact from the mall corridor that visually draws the customer into the store,"* says Debbie Kalisky, Director of Retail Development. *"We*

were challenged by our client to create a unique brand statement and have it executed within the limitations of a very constrained budget. We viewed graphics as a powerful means through which to achieve that."

The bold red and black of the entrance and the cash/wrap area is contrasted with the more sedate white and charcoal floral graphics on the walls — minimizing visual competition for the products below. The white shelves around the perimeter of the store appear to float, almost disappearing as they visually organize the small-scale products and create the illusion of spaciousness — important in a store with only 525 sq. ft. of actual selling space (the entire space is 1000 sq. ft.).

Every inch of space is further maximized with large-scale graphic elements, full-height mirrors, a single large bench and an uncluttered layout.

The bold new image has resonated with customers; the new location has seen a 23% sales increase over the other Brida locations.

Mint Velvet

Chichester, West Sussex, UK

Kinnersley Kent Design
London / Dubai

Handwritten messages add a unique and personal touch to a lighting fixture.

Mint Velvet was founded in 2009 by three women who were frustrated by the lack of affordable, modern clothing that reflected their lifestyle. Kinnersley Kent design was given the task of creating a complete store identity and design for the new brand aimed at women over 30 who wanted easy-to-wear, yet glamorous fashion.

The design concept not only had to work as concession and stand-alone boutique formats, but — adding to the design challenge — it had to be delivered in three months in the most economical way possible in order to give the retailer the best possible chance of succeeding.

Glenn Kinnersley of Kinnersley Kent Design explains, *"The founders' vision is based on 'Looking good, effortlessly.' This theme is embodied everywhere; from the product range where fashion, accessories and knitwear are of a good cut and fit with interesting textures, and an underlying attention to detail, through to the service aspect. For example, shop assistants are called stylists and are trained to advise clients on key pieces and the different ways in which they can be worn. 'Looking good, effortlessly' is the philosophy that unites the brand with the interior. We captured this principle in the store environment. The interior is modern and relaxed, while also tactile and sensuous."*

Several key elements define the Mint Velvet brand and are conveyed in the design and environment. The signature colors of charcoal with highlights of, what else, mint green are found throughout the shop, from the natural grey-washed timber shelving and display tables to the green ticketing.

In another nod to the store name, velvet-lined fixtures lend a touch of glamour to the space, while a

"Style is knowing who you are, what you want to say, and not giving a damn."
GORE VIDAL

TOP: Attention to detail is expressed through little touches such as quotes and small portraits, brass highlights and the "MV" signature, designed by Kinnersley Kent Design, imprinted on tables, cash desks and accessories. **ABOVE RIGHT:** Vintage display cabinets contrast with contemporary modern pieces. **ABOVE LEFT:** Oversized velvet curtains add glamour and soften the mood in the dressing area.

DESIGN
Kinnersley Kent Design
London/Dubai

STORE SIZE
100 m2 (1,076 sq. ft.)

ART DIRECTION
Kinnersley Kent Design

PHOTOGRAPHY
James Winspear

mixture of matt and gloss finishes adds contrast and interest.

Another contrast found in the shop is the eclectic mixture of old and new furniture and props. Carefully selected from different eras and styles, vintage display cabinets contrast with modern pieces designed by Kinnersley Kent Design. Upholstered seating and large mirrors leaning against the walls complete the boutique look and feel of the space.

"Special attention has been paid not only to the look and feel of the store, but also textures, scents and ambience to make customers feel welcome and confident as soon as they walk through the door,"

says Kinnersley.

He continues, *"We delivered a nine month project in three months! We designed the concept, prototyped the fixtures, had it manufactured and installed across two boutique stores and 15 concession in three months on a very limited budget.*

"Our challenge was to achieve that fine balance between creating a relaxed and glamorous environment without being intimidating. We believe we have given it the right 'edge' and confidence to clearly distinguish it from other brands, without shouting about it," finishes Kinnersley.

Judith & Charles

Bayview Village, Toronto, Ontario

GHA design studios

Textured molded fiberglass panels lend a feminine quality to the surrounding architectural surfaces of the façade and a wood entrance portal serves as an elegant transition from mall to boutique.

Judith & Charles, formerly known as Teenflo, was founded in Paris in 1975. In North America, Judith Richardson and Charles Le Pierrès of Montreal have evolved the brand, over the past 20 years, into a preferred line for women seeking quality tailoring, fine fabrics and refined styling. Now with eight locations across Canada and expanding to New York City, Richardson and Le Pierrès asked GHA design studios to give the boutiques a look that would complement the merchandise.

Debbie Kalisky of GHA design studios explains, *"The design mission was to create a modern classic environment that showcases the beautifully tailored garments in an elegant and sophisticated manner. The design concept was inspired by Judith & Charles' collections: simple, exquisite and chic.*

"Their core customer," she continues, *"seeks refinement in her impeccably fitted garments and understands that pieces bought at Judith & Charles are not disposable, but will take her through many seasons. The modern styling and timeless quality are hallmarks of the brand."*

Guided by a philosophy of "less is more" the designers created an colorless architectural envelope within which the merchandise pops. White architectural frames along the walls separate the different collections and allow various merchandising "stories" to be told. The simple layout means that the collections have maximum visibility and are easy to shop.

"The European-inspired visual presentation method is to have all the clothing suspended on hangers with many face-outs," says Kalisky. *"The challenge was to keep the merchandise level dense enough to meet monthly sales expectations, but still be consistent with the merchandise philosophy of not overcrowding the store and retaining its upscale appeal."*

Hardware is finished in a high-quality, brushed stainless steel and concealed wherever possible. Oversized U-bars suspended from within the coves combine with the continuous illumination along the floor platform to give the impression that the clothes are floating in air. The simple shapes and minimalist detailing of the central display tables allow the beauty of the fabrics to shine.

Simplicity of design continues on the ceiling where fully recessed spots set within shallow troughs and continuous linear diffusers allow the sweep of the ceiling to be free of clutter. Framed black-and-white photographs — taken by the owners — sit on an upper ledge, conveying a sense of artistic quality and personal taste. A sense of quality and taste evident throughout the space.

ABOVE: The boutiques straightforward design is characterized by refinement and minimalism, following the brand's philosophy of high quality and elegance. Concealed floor and cove lighting create a glowing box effect. **BELOW:** The minimalism aesthetic extends to the hardware and display fixtures, all of which recede into the background, allowing the various visual merchandising stories to be told.

DESIGN
GHA design studios

STORE SIZE
107 m2 (1,150 sq. ft.)

GENERAL CONTRACTOR
Ing-Pro Development Inc.

LIGHTING DESIGN
Lighting consultant for the general interior store lighting:
Annie Elbaz, Canlyte, Lightolier and Philips

Lighting consultant for the storefront LED strip:
Debra Bouchard, Union Lighting

FIXTURE SUPPLIER
Custom made with Ing-Pro Development Inc.

PHOTOGRAPHER
Philip Castleton

Intermezzo
Huizhou Huamao Place, Huizhou, China

AMS Concept
Shanghai, China

AMS Concept was recently asked to design a modern brand image for IMZ stores in the greater China market; shown here is the launch of the new design. The assignment was to create a unique retail experience that would complement the merchandise and give Intermezzo a premium visual identity — raising consumers' perception of the brand. To do this, the designers used the idea of an "incline" as a springboard to concept the design.

Found throughout the resulting store are oblique angles, strong lines and inclined planes — creating a contemporary space that is attractive to consumers searching for a modern aesthetic in design and clothing.

Display units of sleek black and wood feature vertical lines that form oblique angles with the cement floor, while dark gray light-fixture troughs extend across the ceiling at various angles, two of which lead directly to the large, back-lit branding photo. The unexpected lines and angles give a sense of movement and excitement to the space.

A color palette of dark gray, white and brown serve as a neutral backdrop for the colorful merchandise. The lobby to the fitting rooms is a mirrored box which visually extends the space and eliminates the need to place mirrors in the store itself.

DESIGN
AMS Concept, Shanghai, China

STORE SIZE
109 m2 (1,173 sq. ft.)

FIXTURE, LIGHTING, PHOTOGRAPHY
AMS Concept, Shanghai, China

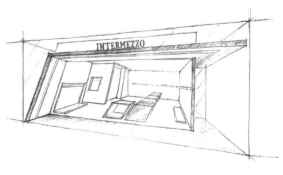

The mirrored lobby to the fitting rooms visually extends the store.

Throughout the space oblique angles and strong lines guide the eye to the merchandise.

Gieves & Hawkes

Shanghai

AMS Concept

Shanghai

Brushed gunmetal was used extensively in the construction of the display window frames and the doorway panels. The new corporate identity color of navy blue is introduced in the glass door header.

Gieves & Hawkes is an international recognized purveyor of English style, with a history of crafts-manship and innovation — the epitome of English excellence in modern-day tailoring which has proudly dressed the Royal monarchy or over 200 years. The retailer recently commissioned AMS Concept to create a new look and image for the retailer's Asian stores that would encapsulate Gieves & Hawkes' new and progressive direction while retaining its quintessential British qualities and characteristics.

For inspiration the designers looked to the retailer's London flagship store located at No. 1 Savile Row in London, the most prestigious tailoring address in the world, a Georgian mansion with authentic architectural elements, but fitted with modern fixtures and furniture. The new AMS design, as seen here in Shanghai, recreates the "rooms" of a mansion — entrance hallway, living room, casual rooms — within a contemporary setting.

In the "entrance hallway" customers are greeted by a modern, brushed gunmetal display table set on classic white-and-black floor tiles. The tiles continue underfoot into the "casual" rooms on either side of the hallway where fixtures, also in brushed gunmetal, have built-in LED strip lighting to illuminate the merchandise. Above each unit, and lending a bit of glamour and star power to the space, are framed photos of celebrities, past and present, who have patronized Gieves & Hawkes.

Gieves & Hawkes are the proud holders of three royal warrants and the brand's close ties to the British Royal Family are evidenced in the transitional area between the casual and formal rooms where a red uniform of the queen's guard is displayed. Customers are also invited to do a bit of Royal watching in the "living" room where a feature wall covered with red wallpaper has more photos, this time of past and present Royals.

The "formal" room replicates a modern gentleman's wardrobe with an elegant display of suits, shirts and pants, and the "personal tailoring service room" offers just what its name implies — the impeccable customer experience and bespoke service upon which Gieves & Hawkes has built its reputation.

ABOVE: The color palette throughout is subtle blues and neutral tones with a splash of red on the "living" room wall.
BELOW: The "formal" room replicates a gentleman's dressing room.

DESIGN
AMS Concept, Shanghai, China

STORE SIZE
110 m2 (1,184 sq. ft.)

FIXTURE, LIGHTING, PHOTOGRAPHY
AMS Concept, Shanghai, China

Myla

JHP Design Consultancy
London

Though the designers at JHP Design Consultancy have designed boutiques and vendor shops for Myla that have appeared in major British department stores, this is the retailer's first flagship store. The luxury brand's shop houses the retailer's new product range in a space that is welcoming and comfortable to shop.

Raj Wilkinson, JHP's Creative Director says, *"The long space we had to work with led us to create a strong, deep store with fitting rooms in the back."* The interior design concept is *"to transport the Myla customer from light to dark — from the light spatial boutique area, echoing the weightlessness of the products, to the richer and darker tones of the bedroom which is more risqué and naughty."*

To introduce the product lines there is a sweeping curved wall with the collection displayed on Nextel coated, steel rails. In the central open space is the store's focal element — a long, narrow table.

Accentuating the importance of the table is a nearly 20-foot-long sculpted chandelier finished with hundreds of acrylic droplets in pink, chocolate and gold. The chandelier, explains Wilkinson, *"adds light and theater to the store's heart. Luxury lined drawers and compartments on the table make* the shopping experience all about engaging with the product."

A custom fixture consisting of a downward spiraling rail supported on a kidney-shaped base is a signature Myla fixture and it appears prominently near the table. The brand's key product lines hang on leather clad straps.

The back wall is more than 12 feet high and covered with bronze-toned mirror panels. A giant curtain of dark plum silk masks the entrance to the opulent and sensuous fitting rooms. Here the walls are upholstered in lavender silk and the gray carpet is echoed in the backlit mirrors. Large scale sensuous imagery, drawn from Myla's ad campaigns, are strategically placed throughout the shop and serve as a guide for the shopper.

Wilkinson says, *"Luxury is inherent in all aspects of the store environment. Silk fabric padded walls, rich colored soft drapery, reflective antiqued mirror surfaces, smoked glass and deep carpeted fitting rooms imbue a sense of 'new boudoir' to the store environment. Apricot mirror glass is used on the long central table, with dark chocolate lacquer, encapsulated with bronze metal, soft cream Nextel curved display rails and rose gold mirrors."* That glam!

OPPOSITE: A custom fixture consists of a downward spiraling rail supported on a kidney-shaped base. **ABOVE:** Large, sensuous imagery, drawn from Myla's ad campaigns, are strategically placed throughout the shop and serve as a guide for the shopper.

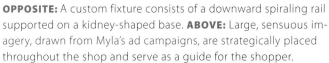

DESIGN
JHP Design Consultancy
London, UK

STORE SIZE
111 m2 (1,200 sq. ft.)

CREATIVE DIRECTOR
Raj Wilkinson

DESIGNER
Helen Sweeney

PHOTOGRAPHY
Adrian Wilson

Peoria Emporium
New York

Peoria Emporium In-house
New York

ABOVE: The main atrium packs a punch of color, clutter, and excitement in the tiniest of spaces. **BELOW:** Shoppers are greeted at the front door by a flat, cutout bust with a hand-painted necklace that proclaims the shop "OPEN." When flipped over, eyes and lips close, the chenille hair goes flat and the necklace changes to "SHUT."

Peoria Emporium is a showcase of unique, one-of-a-kind merchandise within a full-scale contemporary art installation in an antique building in New York City's historic Flatiron District. The store is the natural evolution of two successful enterprises in New York: a shop in Bronxville, and the Tannersville community revitalization Paint Project that used vivid paint colors and graphics on everything from window shutters and trash bins to siding and trim. Designer/owner Elena Agostinis Patterson and her partner, Patricia Grace Stevens, have created a space which has shoppers saying: "I feel as if I've fallen down the rabbit hole!"; "This is like an oasis in the desert!"; "I feel like I've come home!" And, home things will go; if a shopper falls in love with a particular part of the installation, it just might be for sale.

The main focus is ladies' clothing, jewelry, and ac-

cessories. Goods for the home, gifts, and games are included in the mix, with many items designed by the owners and manufactured by women's cooperatives. A signature item, Dinamals, developed by Patricia and found in spots all over the store, is made by, and named for their production associate, Dina Reis. Dear to their hearts are still-lifes created by outsider artist Betty Kuhnel. Other merchandise is imported from such exotic locales as Mali, Burkina Faso, India, Nepal, Peru, Brazil, and Mexico. While price points for clothing range from a few dollars to a few hundred, jewelry and furniture pieces retail for up to $3,000.

"With our demographic between 45 and 85, we think of ourselves as the Anthropologie for Baby Boomers. With income levels ranging from $30,000 to over $1,000,000, our customers seek unique items over designer labels. We attract people with an adventurous spirit… a sense of fun, youthful vigor, and creativity," says Elena.

The eclectic nature of the wares is purposefully echoed by the store's visually exciting sectors of front room, main atrium/stairwell, dressing room, and mezzanine. The ceiling of the front room is a collage of orange and purple t-shirts, cut open at the seams, pleated or bunched as space demands, and stretched

over the entire expanse. High-hat lights, running parallel to the two long walls, peek out through the necks and armholes, casting their light on the displays below. Walls are squares of fake grass, purple bubble wrap covered over with orange plastic construction fencing, and plastic wall planters hung as display racks. The checkout desk is to the right of the entrance. Shoppers are completely enveloped in a wide spectrum of vibrant colors throughout the store's walls, ceilings, fixtures, staircase, and railing. Polka dot multicolored chairs, a vintage toy fire truck being driven by a Dinamal lion, a pedestal lamp painted to look like a skinny model with wide eyes and flame red feather hair—it just goes on and on, never stopping, never missing a beat between selection and presentation.

Varied wall treatments abound in the main atrium. Yellow caution tape, applied in diamond-shape lattice style over a pink painted wall, recalls the era of the 45rpm vinyl record as these 7" discs are used to cover the intersections of the tape. Another wall is painted in pink and yellow floor-to-ceiling stripes. Then, as if not wanting to be outdone by the other two, a lime green third wall with dark-painted vertical-sectioned wood grid has each section filled with various recycled and repurposed items. A full-length shelf over the grid serves as a resting place for a three-dimensional sign, painted red, with small lights placed throughout each letter proclaiming "PEORIA."

The staircase to the mezzanine, another multicol-

ored piece of art, sports a railing, possibly the most unusual focal point of the store. Created by Elena, it evokes the amorphic shape of a multi-tentacled creature ascending the stairs, beckoning shoppers to follow. Grouped on the stairwell wall, offsetting the stairs, a series of "still lifes" by Outsider artist Betty Kuhnel calls shoppers to slow their pace and check them out.

Completing the store is the dressing room area located just beyond the main atrium. Floor-to-ceiling privacy curtains for the two spacious rooms are fabricated from children's t-shirts held together by giant safety pins. Huge mirrors on opposite walls reflect the curtains, making this another festive space. Each room contains a leather chair from Mexico, called an equipale, that has been revitalized with a few coats of vibrant-colored paint and several large dots.

Reminiscent of a 60s poster, a flat cutout bust hanging on the glass-paned entrance door greets shoppers with her short chartreuse "afro" framing her wide-eyed, bubble-gum-pink painted face and parted lips. Her handpainted pectoral necklace in matching green letters proclaims "OPEN"; when flipped over, eyes and lips are closed, the chenille hair is flat, and the necklace proclaims "SHUT." Clearly, creativity, imagination, and ingenuity had free reign in the design of this store.

Bright colors dominate in the dressing rooms with curtains fabricated from children's t-shirts.

The stairwell to the mezzanine.

DESIGN
Peoria Emporium In-house, New York

STORE SIZE
112 m2 (1,200 sq. ft.)

DESIGNER
Elena Agostinis Patterson

LIGHTING
James R. Corbett

CONSTRUCTION MANAGER
Rui Dias

CARPENTRY
Manuel Reis

PHOTOGRAPHY
Bjorn Wallander

The caution-tape wall.

Ecko Unlimited

Rajouri Garden, New Delhi

Future Research Design Company

Bangalore, India

When Ecko Unlimited, licensed from American designer Marc Ecko, recently launched a store in New Delhi, they asked Future Research Design Company (FRDC) of Bangalore to create an environment that would give the *persona* of the brand full expression. This *persona*, or identity, is defined as one of attitude, adventure, non-conforming and artistic — much like Marc Ecko, the founder of the brand. The danger inherent in this directive, according to Sanjay Agarwal, Founder and Director of FRDC was, *"trying to do too many things and failing miserably.*

"Thus, when this international brand came looking for a retail experience," continues Agarwal, *"the call of the day was restraint and experiment on one hand, and yet, on the other, provide a breathtaking and awesome retail experience which stands as a differentiator in the Indian retail market, and provides a befitting canvas for the internationally famous Rhino brand as it started its journey in India."*

Beginning at the store entrance and leading customers into the space is a walkway resembling a catwalk, which then transforms, deeper inside the store, into a "street" for fashion seekers. With the main floor display units situated alongside, the

TOP On the façade, the brackets that enclose the rhino on the logo are transformed into two half brackets that now enclose the window — and the store itself. The window also includes a LCD screen to engage passersby.
ABOVE: Floor fixtures of the brand's signature red give a youthful excitement to the store.

DESIGN
Future Research Design Company,
Bangalore, India

STORE SIZE
115 m2 (1,238 sq. ft.)

DESIGN TEAM
Vineeth, Aditi, Fazal, Sayantani Bhowmick

FIXTURES
Disha Retail Fixtures, Bangalore, India

LIGHTING
Focus Lighting, Mumbai, India

TOP: The angled arrangement of the "walking" shoe display wall illustrates the purpose of the shoes — walking.
ABOVE: The rhino of the logo can be seen everywhere, here on hang tags.

street angles slightly to break up the regular grid of the store and prevent monotony. Customers walking down this street are lead to a life-size rhino, allowing them to become acquainted with, and even touch, the brand logo.

Everything about the appearance of the store is designed to appeal to young and hip men and women 18 to 25 years of age. The high energy of the skateboard culture — unlimited and unbridled — is evoked with colors and graphics, much of it graffiti inspired. The overall black and white color scheme is punctuated with accents of strong red and the bright colors of the merchandise itself.

Framed paintings and brand-centic images are given their own place, high on the walls, creating gallery of paintings that complements the merchandise below and reinforces the brand. The lighting design is tied into this idea of a "gallery" with high intensity lights spotlighting important focal points on the walls and at the displays.

ABOVE: The cash/wrap, seen here in reflection, has watches on display to encourage impulse purchases. **BELOW:** The internal mall entrance — the store is located in City Square Mall — incorporates multiple logos and shallow, but effectively utilized, display windows.

Lakeland Optical

Jackson, Mississippi

Celia Barrett Design, LLC

Jackson, Mississippi/New York

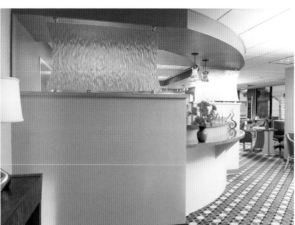

TOP LEFT: Customers entering from the office building are greeted by an Art Deco console and a lit-from-behind blue 3form sign that glows into the night. **TOP RIGHT:** A few steps inside the store, customers are guided into the selling floor by the fluid, gentle curve of a partial wall. Topping this wall is a translucent 3form panel with a wave pattern that, much like a water feature, is both calming and energizing. **ABOVE:** A wall of windows is lined with Fashion Optical fixtures that allow the merchandise to be seen by passersby. The wave in the blue chair fabric reflects the wave in the 3form panels.

DESIGN
Celia Barrett Design, LLC, Jackson, MS/New York, NY

STORE SIZE
121 m2 (1,300 sq. ft.)

FIXTURES
Fashion Optical, Dallas, TX

CONTRACTOR
Heritage Building Corporation, Meridian, MS

PHOTOGRAPHER
Michael Barrett, Barrett Photography, Madison, MS

Lakeland Optical, established in 1978 and well known within the Jackson community, was relocating and needed a total makeover of its store and image. The new location, in Jackson's historic Fondren Arts District, provided the opportunity for the owners to expand their business by attracting the younger crowd that frequents the area. They still needed, however, to appeal to long-standing customers and an older clientele. Celia Barrett Design was asked to design a mid- to upscale image that would fulfill Lakeland's needs.

The new space, on the ground floor of an office building, came with several challenges, including two entrances, one from the street and another from the building lobby, and a long wall of windows that would, if not expertly handled, severely reduce the amount of available display space. Being an optical store also meant that the space had to include a optometrists' work area separate from the selling floor and semi-private consultation areas or "islands" for customers to try on glasses.

"Our goal," states Celia Barrett, *"was to take this iconic local optical store and aid the client in rebranding itself in the trendy art neighborhood of Fondren. The fresh new contemporary design is both whimsical and youthful yet allows a comfortable experience for older customers as well. We also took care to use a few touches of Art Deco to tie the space to the Fondren neighborhood."*

Separating the selling floor from the work area are partial-height walls and a counter with accompanying chairs. Here optometrist can test customers' sight and fit glasses with easy access to the work area behind. Blue, 3form panels top the partial walls and add privacy without having to resort to solid, space-eating walls. The panels also serve to block computer screens from customers' view.

Due to the small space many elements of the design had to serve a dual purpose: cabinets had to both display and store stock, and the selling floor also had to function as a waiting area for service customers. Comfortable, and colorful, seating is provided throughout for this purpose.

Placed in front of the potentially problematic wall of windows are Fashion Optical fixtures that are open at top. These "see through" cases display merchandise while allowing passersby to see into the store.

An overall warm color palette and wood finishes of cherry and maple help to blend the space, and its challenges, into one seamless, and inviting, retail store.

TOP: The main selling area at the rear of the space contains tables for consultations and boutique cabinets that provide both display areas and ample storage. Playful, stylized eyeballs are incorporated into the carpet pattern. **ABOVE:** A curved dropped ceiling soffit follows the curve of the partial wall and counter, adding dimension and interest to the ceiling and further separating the selling space from the optometrists' work area.

Crusoe
Coimbatore, India

Future Research Design Company
Bangalore, India

Brand identification begins on the facade with a "surfable wave."

Crusoe, a maker of men's undergarments headquartered in Coimbatore, India, needed a flagship store that would make a strong impact on potential customers and connect them to the company's already conceived brand ideal of the outdoors man — the adventurer, the explorer, the surfer. Crusoe wanted a store environment that would speak to the overt and latent adventurous streak in every man.

The challenge of creating such a space was given to Future Research Design Company (FRDC) of Bangalore, India. The first hurdle the designers faced was one of perception: the product was men's underwear, after all, a basic wardrobe essential and not always perceived as exciting. How to connect the defined image and the product within a store design that would support both?

It turned out that all the ingredients the designers needed already existed within Crusoe's tagline, "who are you inside." FRDC's strategy was to delve into the defined "spirit of adventure" image to develop the key characteristics that would need to be showcased in the finished design. The resulting space celebrates outdoor pursuits of all sorts, and invites customers to find the adventurous explorer inside themselves. This

adventurer has an up-market slant, however, low-market "rebels" are nowhere in sight.

Of prime importance, once designers had integrated product and image, was to ensure that the store itself stood out from the surrounding clutter in the mall in which it was to be located. For the façade, the designers broke with conventional design and created a huge, wave-like structure — a "surfable wave" — that could not be missed by passersby.

Adding to the spaces distinctiveness are the dim ambient lighting, dark ceiling and earth-toned walls and floor. From the mall aisle the store appears to float in an ocean of darkness. Together, the façade and the lighting create a curiosity point that entices both casual and serious shoppers into the store, increasing traffic and purchases.

Also breaking with convention is the display window, or lack thereof. Right behind the glass are cutouts of surfers — showing the man of action, in action. Although devoid of products these images are full of branding attitude and announce to all that Crusoe is a "World of Adventure." Plans are for the windows to evolve with the season but always convey the same message.

ABOVE AND BELOW: Low ambient light allows the spotlit products and graphics to stand out. Lighting sparkles off the metallic stripes embedded in the floor that radiate from the cash/wrap and lead customers to product zones within the space.

Unique fixtures designed for the space include skate board shelving and lighting fixtures that resemble kayaks.

The man of adventure message continues onto the back wall of the store with a larger-than-life graphic of a rock climber. Everywhere one looks, in fact, there are reminders of the sporting message. Even the type font used throughout — lowercase and bold — appeals to the confident and strong consumer.

The Crusoe product offering includes four core categories: Extreme, Basics, Sports and Next. Within such a small, 130 m2, space ponderous labeling is unnecessary and customers are encouraged to explore and discover each category on their own. Subtle "zoning" is embedded in the floor with metallic strips that radiate from the cash/wrap and direct eye, and foot, movements to the different products.

The design of the fixtures reflects — literally — the adventure sports theme: Wall shelving is shaped like skateboards; stand-alone shelves are in the shape of surfboards. Everywhere one looks there is a reminder of the brand theme, even the suspended track-mounted lighting fixtures resemble kayaks.

Sanjay Agawam, Director of FRDC sums up the design. *"Care has been taken to design a space that does not overpower the merchandise, but creates a context within which the product is celebrated. The props and products are so integrated that the consumer understands that the story telling happening inside the space is actually the story behind the products. So ultimately, the attention shifts to the merchandise.*

"It's as if the energy inherent in the skateboard shelves transfers itself to the products on the shelves; *the surfboard placed casually amidst the merchandise transmits a feeling of the outdoors and fun to the surrounding products; the bike tires and chain convey the passion of a cyclist... all these elements strengthen the association of Crusoe with adventure, leading to brand loyalty."*

With this store, Crusoe has set the benchmark in its retail product category in India, and perhaps soon, outside India as well.

DESIGN/RETAIL CONCEPT/VM DESIGN
Future Research Design Company, Bangalore, India

STORE SIZE
130 m2 (1,400 sq. ft.)

DESIGN TEAM
Sanjay Agarwal, Soma Majumdar, Ruba (Poli Milan), Manoj Raja, Prachi Jain, Sayantani, Aditi D, Tanushree S

CLIENT TEAM
Mr. Abhishek Tibrewal, CMO and Mrs. Ganga Rathna, GM

VISUALIZATION
Fazal and Sanjay U

VM PROPS
Decathlon and Clone Mannequin

FIXTURES AND FURNITURE
Plus, Disha Retail Fixtures, Bangalore, India

LIGHTING
Focus Lighting, Mumbai, India

INTERIOR AGENCY
True Dimensions

ABOVE AND BELOW: Reminders of the adventure-centered brand image can be found everywhere: a motorcycle cutout hovers on a wall; a surfboard anchors the central display; and a rock climber ascends the back wall. All speak to the adventurous spirit within every man.

Paco Rabanne

Alto Las Condes Shopping Center, Santiago

In Store Diseño
Santiago

Paco Rabanne, a French fashion house with its roots in women's fashions, recently decided to enter the South American market and selected Chile as its starting point. The brand hopes to eventually expand into Argentina, Peru and Columbia — all places that Paco Rabanne has had success selling its men's cologne through Falabella, the largest department store in Chile and South America.

Because of its success with men's cologne, particularly in Chile, and its resulting reputation with male consumers, it was decided that for this, its first store in the country, only men's fashions would be sold. The driving concept behind the new store is to fulfill a need for "affordable luxury." The company defines its target audience as young men looking for elegant and refined formal wear and sportswear

The façade is divided in two halves, combining branding and visual merchandising. On the right side, merchandise is showcased in a backless window, while on the left side the company's circular logo appears on a black, highly-reflective surface. Inside the store, the logo appears again, like a beacon, at the end of the central aisle.

The interior is dark and sleek, mixing black fixtures and materials with neutral tans and grays.

FAR LEFT: The fitting rooms are outfitted with lush curtains, upholstered chairs and a modern, grid-patterned mirror. **LEFT:** A grid pattern also appears on the walls behind the fixtures.

with updated and contemporary styling.

Paco Rabanne asked In Store Diseño to create an original retail environment that would embody the spirit of the brand and its history, but within a space dedicated to men. Accomplishing this was a two-fold challenge for the designers. First they worked closely for a year with client personnel to define those iconic elements vital to the brand and its history, but translatable to a masculine environment.

After choosing these elements, the challenge was to contextualize them within a space that would both reiterate the established brand image and attract a sophisticated, international audience — resulting in an exciting new brand experience.

Impeccable visual merchandising, including the display of Paco Rabanne's signature men's colognes, adds an elegance to the space that transcends time and fads while complementing the updated styles.

DESIGN
2008, Patrick Sasmay, In Store Diseño, Santiago, Chile
Paco Rabbane team, Paris, France

STORE SIZE
130 m2 (1,400 sq. ft.)

FIXTURES / LIGHTING
In Store Diseño

PHOTOGRAPHY
Patrick Sasmay

Vespa
Mexico City, Mexico

Plus Construction Group
Tecamachalco, Mexico

ABOVE LEFT: The dramatic and inviting entrance along Masaryk Avenue. **ABOVE RIGHT:** The service desk and large, brand-enforcing graphics are located in the rear of the space.

The mission of the new Vespa shop — located along Masaryk, Mexico City's most important commercial avenue, and designed by Plus Construction Group —is to bring the famous Italian Vespa brand to the entirety of Mexico, not just as a product, but as a lifestyle.

The shop offers not only various versions of the iconic scooter, but a series of related products and accessories such as helmets, jackets, bags, backpacks, gloves, clothing and even souvenirs such as pins and to-scale scooter models. Expert advice is also on offer and a service department is located on the lower level. Although the whole concept is primarily targeted to customers between the ages of 30 and 40, when selling a classic brand such as Vespa, older customers are always part of the mix.

The main challenge for the designers was to finely balance the classic aspects of the brand with contemporary design and styling and create a concept for the new space that would reflect the brand and communicate the Vespa lifestyle to the shopping public. Another, very down-to-earth challenge, was the time frame within which the project was developed — two months.

Informing every aspect of the design is the mixture of retro and contemporary styles inherent in the product itself. Tradition materials such as the walnut found in the furniture and the natural stone of the floor are contrasted with simple forms, straight lines and minimalist finishes. At the entrance sleek black granite and overhanging black rafters are complemented by the organic shape and rough bark of a nearby tree.

To best utilize the small, 130 m2 space the designers looked to an Italian town or villa for inspiration. A central "street" runs down the middle of the store along which the Vespas are positioned, lending their own classic design to the ambience of the interior. Architectural details on the walls, suggestive of Italian architecture, gracefully frame display furniture and large, brand-centric graphics.

The street metaphor continues right onto the back wall where a large image of an Italian street, and the Vespa logo, is located. Also in the back of the store is the customer service desk complete with contemporary and stylish chairs.

The Sheetrock ceiling is designed to impart a strong sense of perspective to the space as seen from the entrance. Dropped panels on either side of the space lead the eye directly down the line of colorful scooters. Direct and indirect lighting mix to dramatically showcase the products.

The concept, which won honorable mention at the International Design Awards, will be carried into future projects developed by Vespa.

The small space is given depth by the strong sense of perspective created by the ceiling

DESIGN
Plus Construction Group, Tecamachalco, Mexico

STORE SIZE
130 m2 (1,399 sq. ft.)

DESIGN/ARCHITECTURE
Carlos Carreño Cano

PROJECT MANAGER
Carlos Carreño Cano

DIRECTOR OF DESIGN PRODUCTION
Arturo Cole

PRINCIPAL IN CHARGE
Eduardo Sosa

BUILDING CONTRACTOR
Plus Construction Group, Tecamachalco, Mexico

FIXTURES/LIGHTING
Plus Construction Group, Tecamachalco, Mexico

PHOTOGRAPHY
Courtesy of the designers

Jones Bootmaker

Milton Keynes, UK

Dalziel and Pow Design Consultants

London/Mumbai/Shanghai

The recently launched new look of Jones Bootmaker — designed by Dalziel and Pow Design Consultants — is a progression from the brands trademark green and pink color scheme and draws inspiration from an aesthetic of "tone and texture." A new store in Milton Keynes, shown here, showcases the new stylish and simplified direction of the brand.

The history of Jones Bootmaker reaches back to 1857 when Alfred Jones and his wife Emma opened a shop in Bayswater, London. Even then, the retailer was eager to embrace the newest in interior innovations: the Jones' shop was one of the first in the area to install electric light. A huge draw at the time.

Present day innovations are intended to draw customers with brand recognition. The new tonal "white box" architecture of this 135 m2 space allows the portfolio of brands carried by Jones Bootmaker to be presented with visual clarity and versatility.

Fully flexible shelving, alongside fixed feature walls, allows the retailer to introduce new brands with ease and to vary the product mix seasonally.

Says Keith Ware, Group Director, *"Visual merchandising techniques will be varied, adding more visual interest to the presentation of the product. The central units have also been redesigned, to allow more flexible layouts and maximise circulation space for ease of shopping."*

Textured carpet and luxurious chrome and bronze metal finishes on fixtures are mixed with leather furniture to create a more upscale shopping environment without repositioning the brand or raising price points.

Ware concludes. *"The overall experience and aim of the new Jones Bootmaker store concept is to present the brand's signature, expertly-crafted collections in a refreshingly contemporary and versatile environment — to create a luxurious, unrushed retail experience."*

DESIGN
Dalziel and Pow Design Consultants
London/Mumbai/Shanghai

STORE SIZE
135 m2 (1,453 sq. ft.)

Inspiration for the new look of the shop is drawn from an architectural aesthetic of "tone and texture."

styled by me™ Barbie®

New York

Mattel, Inc.
El Segundo, CA

The interaction of the touch screen kiosks connects directly to the world in which the girls live. Their familiarity with the technology, usually greater than that of their mothers', gives them a sense of command over the experience.

The 139 m2 (1,500 sq. ft.) styled by me Barbie located in FAO Schwarz's Fifth Avenue store in New York City is truly unique. Here, in an elegant, special boutique created by Mattel, Inc., girls can customize their own Barbie dolls and then watch them "walk" down a doll-sized runway in a dramatic fashion show.

Kim Helgeson, Visual Merchandising Manager for Mattel, explains, *"The moment they arrive, girls of all ages will be captivated by two large Barbie doll styling stations, complete with eight interactive touch screens that guide girls through a step-by-step design process to personally select a doll, fashions, accessories, a doll case and even a gift for themselves."* They can choose from among seven different Barbie dolls and friends featuring different skin tones, hair colors and styles. *"After styling out their Barbie dolls, girls can debut their*

The look of the styling stations, while high-tech, is modified with soft lighting and ice cream cone shapes to appeal to young girls.

In the middle of the store, a large dome covers the doll-sized fashion runway. Large monitors flank the stage, floating on frosted acrylic off-set on pink floral wallpaper. Hip, fast-paced music keeps the tempo of the runway show production. Small led lights flash while clicking "camera" noises accompany the newly-styled doll as she struts the runway.

The gentle curves of the cash wrap is reflected in the graceful legs of the furniture. Round shapes throughout the decor contrast with the horizontal and angled lines that define the space.

DESIGN
Mattel, Inc., El Segundo, CA

STORE SIZE
139 m² (1,500 sq. ft.)

STORE DESIGNER &
PROJECT MANAGER
Kim Helgeson, Visual Merchandising Manager, Mattel, Inc.

FIXTURES/SIGNAGE
Greneker Solutions,
Los Angeles, CA
Creative Forces, Monrovia, CA
Spark Retail Solutions,
Huntington Beach, CA

PHOTOGRAPHY
John Fleck, Indianapolis, IN

newly styled doll in a mini fashion show in which each customized Barbie doll will appear from behind a screen, 'walk' down the miniature working runway and, ultimately, strike a pose for her audience." Using fun animation and music, the dolls are seen on the two large screens on either side of the runway.

The space is dominated by the blushing pink color that is synonymous with Barbie and Barbie packaging. White fixtures and the dark brown wood floor form a neutral backdrop for the colorful merchandise while a pink floral pattern on the walls is repeated in "etched" floral patterns on glass side panels and pink floral stool cushions. With additional feminine touches such as fashion sketches in ornate silver frames and a pink chandelier, the space becomes a world apart for the young girls who find

their way up to the second level of FAO Schwarz.

"Establishing a balance between the various looks of feminine sophistication, youthful whimsy and high-tech was important to the design," concludes Helgeson. *"This balance was created with the use of color, shape and texture. The use of these multi-sensory elements creates an atmosphere that appeals to both girls and mothers."*

This space was recognized with several design awards including an Award of Merit from the Institute of Store Planners & VMSD; Outstanding Merit from A.R.E. Design Awards; and a Gold Award from *Design of the Times.*

Kidrobot

South Beach, Miami

MASHstudios
Los Angeles

ABOVE: The space seen from the back of the shop. The designers were not able to change the facade, or enlarge the small front window due to the location's historical zoning. Along the wall apparel is keep in order and indexed by special hang bars. **LEFT:** The front column with its integrated shoe display. The graphic on the wall is by French street artist, Tilt.

Founded in 2002 by designer Paul Budnitz, Kidrobot is the world's premier creator of limited edition art toys and apparel. The company creates toys, apparel, accessories, and other products in collaboration with many of today's top artists and designers, exemplifying the cutting edge of both pop art and mass culture.

Many of Kidrobot toys such as Dunny, MUNNY, and Frank Kozik's Labbits and Mongers, attract huge followings, and artists that work with Kidrobot often gain celebrity status. Kidrobot also regularly collaborates with many of the world's top brands to create unique, limited-edition products. Past collaborations include Marc Jacobs, Visionaire Magazine, Barneys New York, The Standard Hotels, Playboy, Burton and Nike.

A blend of sculpture and popular art, many of the exclusive toys are extremely rare and collectible. Kidrobot toys retail anywhere from $5 to $25,000 and many appreciate in value over time. In 2006, Kidrobot launched its exclusive apparel line. Vibrant, distinctive and produced in limited runs, the apparel draws its inspiration from the company's unique pop art aesthetic.

Stores are located in New York City, London, San Francisco, Los Angeles, and Miami, seen here and designed by MASHstudios of Los Angeles. The direc-

Figurines and toys are displayed in cabinets behind sliding glass doors and illuminated with concealed lighting.

tive for Kid Robot Miami was to create a fresh, fun environment that was exciting and hip but still sleek enough to flow seamlessly with the eclectic merchandise.

Bernard Brucha of MASHstudio explains, *"Kid Robot carries an array of products, from miniature collectables to apparel, so it was important to fashion the perfect backdrop for items, big and small, to sit side-by-side. One of the store's signature lines include 2.5 inch-tall figurines, so one goal was to play up the importance of all these tiny pieces. Sleek shelving, compartments, cases and platforms — all with low, horizontal profiles — achieved this effect, leaving the space feeling clean but not clinical."*

Lighting was a challenge due to the small windows and hurricane constraints — the store is one block from South Beach. To address the problem, and open up the shop, the designers created false "skylights" by cutting openings in the central ceiling structure. These openings are exactly the same size as the display units sitting directly below and wrapped in the

same vinyl — giving the effect that the display units have been lowered, or dropped, from the ceiling.

Another challenge arouse from time constraints. *"Lead-time was super tight,"* says Brucha, *"we were working on the San Francisco store when we received the call and had three weeks to concept and five weeks to build and install the millwork.*

"Managing the chaos was the main objective," he continues. *"There were thousands of toys to be displayed. We needed to display them in a way that made each item important but not precious. The collectables are special but not unobtainable. Throw in a client that's also a designer and it makes for a fun collaboration!"*

The finished, streamlined design mixes with the pops of color from the brand's signature merchandise to maintain the vibe of the previous Kidrobot stores while giving the Miami location its own vibrant identity.

The cash/wrap with the giant Dunny neon sign that has became standard in all Kidrobot stores. False skylights were created by cutting openings in the ceiling the same size as the displays below and wrapping both in the same vinyl.

DESIGN
MASHstudios, Los Angeles, CA

STORE SIZE
141 m2 (1,520 sq. ft.)

CUSTOM MILLWORK / CUSTOM LIGHTING
MASHstudios, Los Angeles, CA

PHOTOGRAPHY
Mike Butler

Worth Avenue News

West Palm Beach, Florida

PDT International

Fort Lauderdale, Florida

Worth Avenue News is a "news and gifts" concept store developed by PDT International and located in The Paradies Shops in Palm Beach International Airport. The shop offers a large selection of local apparel, gifts and accessories showcased in a design that references the legendary lifestyle of Palm Beach.

The assignment was to create a space that pays homage to the well-known, historic shopping district of Worth Avenue in Palm Beach originally designed by Addison Mizner, an architect best known for his Mediterranean Revival and Spanish Colonial Revival architecture. The façade of Worth Avenue News takes its architectural cues from its famous namesake, and lantern sconces flank both the main, and secondary entrances, creating a street-like feel from the corridor.

The store's design is inspired by the rich history of Palm Beach and the architectural style of Addison Mizner. Light from the atrium that encloses the store streams through the open beam ceiling.

DESIGN
PDT International,
Fort Lauderdale, FL

STORE SIZE
148 m2 (1,591 sq. ft.)

FIXTURES
Windsor Fixtures

LIGHTING
PDT International
E. Sam Jones

FAUX PALM TREES
Treescapes International

PHOTOGRAPHY
Dana Hoff

The store is located within the airport's atrium where an abundance of natural light streams through the space. To take advantage of this light and maintain the openness of the atrium, an open beam ceiling was designed that utilizes distressed beams in rich mahogany. The open ceiling design, in turn, necessitated the addition of four, eight-inch square posts for structural support. The designers clad these posts in life-like palm trees that tower over customers and recreate the lush landscaping found along the Worth Avenue promenade.

The store's color palette is a rich tapestry of terracotta, plum and copper. Warm terracotta floors are softened with Mexican tile pavers and merchandise is displayed on patina-aged fixtures. Above the centrally located cash/wrap is suspended a large, wrought iron chandelier, another reference to the rich style of historic Worth Avenue and Palm Beach.

Americanino

Mall Plaza Calama, Santiago

In Store Diseño

Santiago

An industrial, urban ambiance is introduced on the store's facade and continues onto the back wall where a "window" presents the New York City skyline and the brand's signature jeans are displayed.

Americanino is a relatively new brand geared to young men and women looking for hip, casual trends with a vintage feel. Best know for its brand of jeans, Americanino recently challenged itself to climb to the next level of brand positioning and establish itself in a store that would be instantly recognizable as *the* place for young people seeking an urban lifestyle.

In Store Diseño of Santiago was charged with developing a design concept in which customers could identify themselves with the icons of an idealized urban environment. The resulting store, shown here in the Mall Plaza Calama, evokes a New York industrial, loft-style apartment.

The look is introduced on the façade where metal and brick are utilized to recreate an old building with the security gates partially lifted, as might be found in an industrial or old section of New York City.

On the rear wall of the space is replicated a factory "window," complete with images of the city's famous skyline — connecting the urban image to the products displayed immediately in front of the window. Modular, metal panels and fixtures allow these displays to be rearranged.

Along the sides of the shop, merchandise is presented as if in the closet of the imaginary occupants of the "loft apartment." Materials and props found throughout the store — brick walls, concrete finishing, wooden tables — all deliver a consistent, urban image. The vintage look and industrial-like experience is further enhanced with dim, warm lighting.

Props found throughout the space reinforce the urban, industrial-loft apartment that the design evokes.

DESIGN
2011, Amalia Pérez and Rosa Astorga, In Store Diseño, Santiago, Chile

STORE SIZE
150 m2 (1,614 sq. ft.)

FIXTURES/LIGHTING
In Store Diseño

PHOTOGRAPHY
In Store Diseño

2011, Amalia Pérez and Rosa Astorga, In Store Diseño, Santiago, Chile

Bernard Weatherill

Savile Row, London

Dalziel and Pow Design Consultants

London/Mumbai/Shanghai

Bernard Weatherill, a famous country and equestrian tailoring house, provides a bespoke service as well as luxurious ready-to-wear clothing and accessories. When the brand recently relaunched with a new flagship store on Savile Row in London, Dalziel and Pow Design Consultants was charged with creating a new brand identity, store design, packaging and art direction. Neil Speller, Team Leader, Interiors, says, *"Previously available only as bespoke, the brand has built on its impeccable credentials to expand its offering, providing the finest range of country and equestrian wear to the most discerning customers in the world."*

Founded in 1910, Bernard Weatherill was established on Savile Row by 1912. Since the '20s the company has had a Royal Warrant to provide riding clothes to the Royal Family including, today, Her Majesty the Queen — discerning customers indeed.

"The new store creates a very distinctive retail identity for Bernard Weatherill" says Speller, *"combining traditional vintage shopfittings in a clean contemporary space. Strong color, eclectic furniture and premium materials are used, to create a unique home for the brand."*

The façade presents a restraint typical of Savile Row, with a hint of the product offering provided by a full-size sculpted horse in the window.

Inside, space is divided into clear zones — menswear,

womenswear and accessories — plus a very generous fitting area. Traditional rugs differentiate the zones, creating "rooms" within the 150 m2 store. Further defining the space, the ceilings are wallpapered in a custom hand-printed paper applied to simple planes. The floor is generally limestone with a coir matting in the service area, and shopfittings are a combination of new minimal blackened steel wall frames and reclaimed, renovated antique furniture.

Speller concludes, *"The fashionably eclectic mix of styles and periods suits the heritage of the brand and introduces a new fresh outlook for the future."*

Traditional rugs differentiate the shop's zones and renovated antique furniture adds an elegant touch. **ABOVE RIGHT:** The fitting rooms are four times the size of those of a typical fashion store, allowing for measuring and fitting of the bespoke tailoring.

DESIGN
Dalziel and Pow Design Consultants
London/Mumbai/Shanghai

STORE SIZE
150 m2 (1,615 sq. ft.)

holpe+

Hau Qiang Bei, Shenzhen, Guangdong Province, PR China

rkd retail/iQ

Bangkok/Shenzhen/Shanghai

The new holpe+ store launches the new environment for the brand, including signature colors and graphic communications.

DESIGN
rkd retail/iQ, Bangkok, Shenzhen, Shanghai

CLIENT TEAM
Shenzhen Holpe Commercial Chain Stock

STORE SIZE
150 m2 (1,615 sq. ft.)

PHOTOGRAPHER
Pruk Dejkamhang

The new holpe+ store shown here is a market segmentation of holpe, the leading telecommunication retailer in Guandong Province, China. Currently operating more than 300 locations the parent brand, holpe, is primarily product-driven and offers little in the way of retail experience. It has, however, some clear core competencies and advantages, not least of which is a reputation for excellent customer service. These competencies could not be lost in holpe+ but brought forward and strengthened.

rkd retail/iQ, the designers of the new brand, explains, *"holpe+ was created as a market differentiation and brand building segmentation format for Holpe. An extraordinary assortment of mobile technology, accessories and telecom and customer services were all combined within a wholly new retail planning and design concept specifically targeted to key customer groups: fashion and business. The marketing strategy is based on an edited assortment and superior services, and not price. The real estate strategy of Holpe had been on the high street and had not yet had moved inside the upscale*

ABOVE AND BELOW: Of central importance to the visual merchandising of the new space is the open presentation of telephones and accessories, a departure from traditional showcase presentation. Mid-floor fixtures incorporate lighting elements that draw in customers and unify the multi-brand displays. End caps showcase key product launches and complete accessory solutions.

An undulating ceiling is punctuated with linear reveals and accent lighting fixtures. Additional lighting emanates from various sources to create an inviting environment.

shopping centers. Retail developers who were previously not accepting of the Holpe retail concept in their developments have all expressed keen interest the new holpe+ format."

The design of holpe+ incorporates cutting-edge, interactive technology into key fixtures, enabling customers to enhance their mobile service on an ongoing basis through touch screens and wireless connections. Customer service is further improved with the introduction of the "plus club." This area within the store offers "chill" and "download" zones as well as complete customer service.

A dramatic, sculptural feature wall stretches from the entrance to the rear of the store and holds new merchandise and integrated business solutions.

rkd retail/iQ was responsible for the strategic brief and all creative expressions including name generation, brand and environmental graphics, retail planning and design, and is currently rolling out the program across multiple locations in southern China.

The area of the shop designated "plus club" offers download zones, seating and complete service-provider enrollment.

Brand-building graphics and signage are introduced in the store and can be found throughout the space.

Desa

St. Martins Courtyard, Covent Garden, London

Kinnersley Kent Design
London / Dubai

Careful attention to details supports the Desa philosophy of "Innovation through tradition."

Desa, a maker of premium leather goods, recently wanted to enter the UK market — a market where it was largely unknown. Founded in Turkey in 1972, Desa had more than 70 stores internationally and employed craftsmen that produced leather goods for some of the world's finest luxury labels.

Kinnersley Kent Design was asked to create an elegant and intimate retail environment that would position Desa in the UK as an aspirational luxury leather and fashion house, with luxury handbags, leather garments, footwear, knitwear and fashion at its core.

"When introducing a brand into a region for the first time, it is vital to ensure that the offer is adapted properly to fit the local market. Our aim was therefore to position Desa so that prospective customers understand what it sells, what's unique about it and give them a reason to choose Desa over other luxury brands. Our aim was to create an elegant, glamorous and stylish retail environment that celebrates Desa's heritage of quality, craftsmanship and design, with the product as hero." explains Lindie Champion of Kinnersley Kent Design.

The color pallet of muted, warm tones with highlights of brass, marble and leather, and the dark, oak herringbone flooring bring warmth and elegance to the store — a space designed to appeal women, Desa's first target customer in the UK. The theatrical lighting is focused on the products rather than the walkways and custom-made display cabinets reflect the traditional craftsmanship of the merchandise.

Champion says, *"We believe that we have successfully created a luxurious, yet understated environment that presents Desa's products in the best possible light. Part of the brief was that the developed design concept should be easy to execute, work in both boutique and flagship formats, so that the concept positions itself as an attractive investment opportunity for future growth to locations such as Paris and New York, making Desa a truly international leather and fashion house."*

TOP RIGHT: Leather clad pilasters complete with stitched leather detailing contain recessed display cases that showcase products as if they were museum pieces. Lined with bronze mirrors each has its own integral lighting. **ABOVE:** Brass is used extensively, it covers the edges of shelves, and plates of brass hide hanging rails.

DESIGN
Kinnersley Kent Design, London/Dubai

STORE SIZE
160 m2 (1,722 sq. ft.)

ART DIRECTION
Kinnersley Kent Design

SHOPFITTER
KAD Retail

PHOTOGRAPHER
Peter Cook

Euro-Optica
Madrid

MARKETING-JAZZ
Madrid

For over 30 years Euro-Optica has been a fixture in the Majadahonda district of Madrid. Recently the noted optician moved into an available adjacent space and added Euro-Sone, a hearing center, to the shop. The retailer called upon Carlos Aires of MARKETING-JAZZ to create a new concept that would incorporate both elements into the new space.

"The challenge lay in designing an innovative shop that would bring together the two brands — Euro-Optia and Euro-Sone — under the same roof," states Aires. *"We had to do this with clear, recognizable unity, to combine the atmosphere, the shop design and the product presentation into a single experience. We were after visual excitement — a contagious energy."*

Aires did not consider this just an interior design project but one of *"creative visual marketing."* He needed to design a shopping space that would

ABOVE: Customers are directed from the reception desk to either Euro-Optica to the right or Euro-Zone up the stairs.
BELOW: The tables and chairs of the Euro-Optica zone of the store.

To accommodate those who wait for personalized service, there are white plastic and stainless chairs accented with the green color on both levels of the shop.

accommodate the product offering and also afford the shopper a comfortable and convenient place to interact with the product. Amongst the challenges facing the designer was the need to underscore the brand's attributes such as quality, innovation and personalized service — in an environment that was "accessible and unpretentious."

The simple white stone facade accommodates the store's location on a graded plot. Since there is an up-slant, the designer was able to create a mezzanine within the shop. The optical area is at entrance level while the hearing department, readily visible upon entering the store, is up a few steps.

The interior glistens in its whiteness — off white walls, floors, ceiling and white laminate-covered fixtures and white plastic chairs. The space also appears more spacious than its 160 m2 thanks to a large amount of clear glass and carefully located panels of mirror. Accenting all this clean whiteness is a sharp yellow-green color — the color of the store's

logos — combined with black. The new logos were also designed by MARKETING JAZZ.

The reception desk is near the entrance and shoppers are directed from there to the desired service. The Euro-Optica space is to the right of the desk. It includes several individual stations with plastic and glass tables and light-looking chairs with the signature green seat covers.

In keeping with the light and airy look of the store, the frosted glass steps that lead to the hearing department on the mezzanine are illuminated from below and the side panels are translucent plastic encased within stainless steel rails.

This prototype has proven so successful that the client is now preparing to roll out the concept in other parts of Madrid.

DESIGN
MARKETING-JAZZ, Madrid

STORE SIZE
160 m2 (1,690 sq. ft.)

CREATIVE DIRECTOR AND
FURNITURE DESIGN
Carlos Aires

ILLUSTRATOR
Elena de Andres

3D GRAPHICS
Alejandro Andreu

GRAPHIC DESIGN/
CORPORATE IDENTITY
Natalia Sanchez de Pedro

CONSTRUCTION
**Daniel Lopez,
Construcciones DASO**

LIGHTING
**Nuria Torrents,
Microlights Espagna**

PHOTOGRAPHER
**Luis Sanchez de Pedro Aires,
Aires Photography Studio**

BELOW: The overall white interior is punctuated by the signature color of bright green.

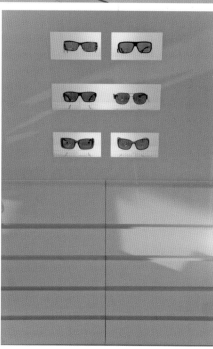

Jaeger London

St. Martins Courtyard, Covent Garden, London

Kinnersley Kent Design

London / Dubai

White ceramic flooring, off-white chalk walls and the exposed ceiling with hanging raft serve as a neutral backdrop for the merchandise.

Jaeger, a British fashion brand established in 1884 and renowned for its innovative and stylish fashion, accessories and home wear, asked Kinnersley Kent Design to create a freestanding boutique to house the Jaeger London collection — a line inspired by, and expanded from, the retailer's catwalk collection.

The designers were charged with creating a boutique format that would appeal to the fashion-aware, urban, working woman who appreciates quality and design. The concept needed to appeal broadly to lifestyle rather than age and reflect Jaeger's brand values of quality, luxurious fabrics and attention to detail, set in a relaxed environment.

Glenn Kinnersley explains, *"As the label stands for female-friendly, practical, Anglo-centric cool, our aim was to reflect this philosophy in the interior. The result is a contemporary environment with a traditional twist."*

Elegant and simple interior elements include dark oak, timber-framed fixtures that appear to be casually propped against the wall. These fixtures serve to frame the merchandise and create outfit-building display areas while providing flexibility.

Distinctive details such as custom-made paneling on key walls and lighting fixtures that resemble bare bulbs hanging from the ceiling contribute a hip, urban-loft feel without detracting from the soft, feminine quality of the boutique.

"The idea behind the concept was to give a sense of space, a clean, light backdrop and gallery inspired environment with a contemporary, modern interpretation of classic style and quality," says Kinnersley.

The first boutique in Covent Garden, shown here, was followed by boutiques in Canary Wharf and Leadenhall Market — both in the UK. Typical store size is 160 m2.

ABOVE LEFT: The lighting fixture above the cash/wrap amasses the light fixtures that appear singly throughout the store.

ABOVE RIGHT: The dark oak staircase features nickel in-lay and the paneling detail with unique molding.

DESIGN
Kinnersley Kent Design, London/Dubai

STORE SIZE
160 m2 (1,722 sq. ft.)

ART DIRECTION
Kinnersley Kent Design

SHOPFITTER
Esprit UK Ltd

PHOTOGRAPHER
Peter Cook

ABOVE RIGHT: Furniture includes pieces from contemporary British designers, such as Tom Dixon's wingback chair and Benjamin Hubert's "pebble" stool seen here in a fitting room.

Yusty

Zielo de Pozuelo Shopping Center, Madrid

MARKETING-JAZZ

Madrid

TOP LEFT: The display window that was the inspiration for the new store design. **TOP RIGHT:** The facade of the new in-mall shop.
ABOVE AND OPPOSITE: The cubic aspect of the design can be seen everywhere in the clean, white space.

Carlos Aires of MARKETING-JAZZ was awarded the contract to design the new in-mall space for menswear retailer, Yusty, because of a plan he devised that was based on a window display he had designed for the retailer's original store in Madrid. Two aspects of that window display made their way into the design for the new store. The first were the cubes of various sizes and heights that filled the window, some holding merchandise; the second was a perimeter of lighting running horizontally around the window.

The cubic elements in the store design can be seen everywhere one looks. The furniture, display cases and shelving units all contain cubes of various heights and arrangements. Wall units — both white and black — incorporate neat grids of display niches, and modular platforms, again in variations on the cubic theme, add flexibility to the visual merchandising.

The perimeter lighting of the original window reappears in the store design as a lighting tube that runs horizontally around the shop at the top of the wall displays. Additional lighting is provided by overhead spots and lighting that originates from the base of some of the display cases.

Customer service is one of Yusty's key values, and a central customer service area, that includes the cash/wrap, divides the shop into front and back areas. In addition to the front, mall-facing display window, there are five internal display areas. These in-store displays showcase arrangements of mannequins and merchandise — always in harmony with the front display.

Attention to detail, the open space and a limited color palette serve to create a look of sophistication and modernity.

Display cases are the result of designer Carlos Aires' "cubic" inspiration for the store. The units start with a grid pattern, but mix in cases of various sizes, creating visual interest.

DESIGN
MARKETING-JAZZ, Madrid

STORE SIZE
160 m2 (1,690 sq. ft.)

CREATIVE DIRECTOR AND
FURNITURE DESIGN
Carlos Aires

ILLUSTRATION AND SKETCHES
Elena de Andres

PHOTOGRAPHER
Luis Sanchez de Pedro Aires,

TOP: The back part of the shop. **ABOVE RIGHT:** The cubic elements of the design are everywhere. **ABOVE LEFT:** The centrally-located cash/wrap.

Full Circle

Brinkworth

London

The Full Circle brand is defined, in this new store by a huge, eye-catching circle — the dynamic focal point of the design. Adam Brinkworth of Brinkworth, describes the store's design as *"a floating white architectural box, set within an envelop of the original landlord's space, that has been cut away to reveal a dramatic optical illusion that — when viewed from the shop entrance — describes a 12-meter-wide, full circle at the rear of the shop."* The distinction between the floor, walls and ceiling are blurred in the stark contrast of overlapping materials and colors.

A similar dramatic effect has been created on exiting the shop, with the use of one-way reflective film, applied to the shop window. The optical illusion of both "full circles" can only be viewed — complete — from specific standpoints in the store —

distorting as the shopper moves from that position. The cash desk and the supporting column, both finished in black stainless steel, shimmer within the black circle set against rough rendered walls. Glowing circular halo lights on the floor surround the mannequins that are set on the store's actual floor level — to reiterate the full circle theme and affect a contrast between the envelop and the new addition.

Men's fashions are located on the right-hand side of the shop and the wall is constructed with large wardrobe-like frames — angled away from the entrance — *"to maintain the architectural aesthetic inside the store."* These units are made of a combination of crisp, polished Carrera marble and white armour coat. They have stainless steel rails and curved shelves of smoked glass. The frames that wrap

around to the rear of the space become the cubicles that serve as the men's dressing rooms.

The left wall, for women's wear, has a warmer and softer feel with gray stone and sand stone laid in a brick-like linear fashion. The modular units combine front- and side-out hanging on stainless steel rails that have integral lighting. The women's changing rooms are behind the big black circle and they have felt-lined walls with silk-lined wool curtains and large halo-lit oak framed mirrors that lean against the rough render walls.

"The men's and women's collections are delineated on either side of the store through the contrasting yet complementary materials palette, while contemporary and beautifully detailed fixtures and furniture share this palette and unite the two areas seamlessly," explains Brinkworth. The unusual pieces of furniture and accessories by British designers — provided by twentytwentyone — *"underpin the British ethos that lies at the core of the Full Circle brand."*

LEFT: The women's changing rooms have felt-lined walls with silk-lined wool curtains and large halo-lit oak framed mirrors leaning against the rough render walls.
OPPOSITE: The cash desk and the supporting column, both finished in black stainless steel, shimmer within the black circle set against rough rendered walls.

DESIGN
Brinkworth, London, UK

DESIGNERS
Adam Brinkworth, Andrew Shove, David Hurren, Bodrul Khalique

STORE SIZE
163 m2 (1,754 sq. ft.)

CONTRACTOR
Syntec

PHOTOGRAPHY
Alex Franklin

Verona Vibe

Les Galeries de Hull, Quebec

Ruscio Studio
Montréal

Verona Vibe, a shoe retailer with in-mall stores throughout the greater metropolitan Montréal area, recently called upon Ruscio Studio to help with an ambitious expansion. The retailer wanted to expand into preferred locations in prime centers and broaden their product offering to include men's shoes. They also planned on targeting a specific demographic — young, hip 20- to 30-year-olds — and compete head on with Spring, the top retailer in the low- to mid-market shoe category and a division of Aldo shoes.

To do all of this Verona Vibe needed a complete makeover. As Robert Ruscio, President of Ruscio Studio explains, *"Their store concept was basic, bland, seemed to address too general of a demographic, and did not make a lasting impression. It seemed like the only asset for the retailer was low pricing and vast assortment."*

Verona Vibe needed a new concept that would differentiate them from all other stores and add a sense of fashion and value to the brand. And, as they would be introducing new, name-brand lines to the store, consideration had to be given to properly showcase the hot, trend-setting merchandise,

"We knew the brand required a sharper focus on its

The floor displays and base of the curved shelves have the same treatment, integrating well with each other.

primary target market, a younger, hip clientele," Ruscio continues. "Our greatest challenge, however, was the budget. An aggressive multiple store expansion meant that we had to do more with less. We had to rely on our creativity and work with the basic elements, such as color, contrast and even laminates. We needed to achieve a 'bang for the buck.' We had to also consider that the general contractor was likely to be the lowest bidder with limited resources. Therefore, the design had to be easy to interpret and simple to build."

The first thing one notices about the new design is the color red. It's everywhere — flooring, walls, ceiling, logo — all are red. It's impossible to walk by the store and not notice it or to feel indifference toward it. Ruscio states, "Several meetings were required to convince the client that an entirely red store would not distort the color of the goods. Persuading him to invest in quality lighting and a few 'trust us' statements

allowed us to prevail in the end."

To make the look work, however, all the reds — the marmoleum flooring, plastic laminate, paint and acrylic — had to match, otherwise the concept would be compromised. Since color selection in the marmoleum can be restrictive, it was the first material selected and, because it lends itself to creating a joint-less, monolithic finish, it was also wrapped on several vertical surfaces to integrate floor and fixtures. This idea of seamlessness is also incorporated at the cash/wrap area where the floor appears to curve up into the cash/wrap unit.

All the "branded" items are located on the left side of the store within a white wall unit and labeled with tabs that highlight the brands. Other, "unbranded" merchandise is displayed on the curved shelves on the right side of the store. These curved shelves, consistent with the curves found elsewhere in the store, have deeper shelves near the floor and thinner shelves at top, making them ergonomically comfortable to shop. Additionally, as the product offering expands and contracts from season to season the continuous shelving gives flexibility to the merchandise display.

One of the few elements in the store not red are the large branding images of hip young people. These black-and-white cut-out graphics states Ruscio, *"are essential elements as they help to instantly define the store brand and are visually powerful against the bold red background. By applying the large 'lifestyle' visuals directly on the walls, emphasis is placed on the brand experience rather than the product only."*

The new façade frames the store in simple white, placing emphasis on the bold, red interior and allowing the entire product offering to be seen at a glance. The store name, in addition to being seen overhead, is placed at eye-level on both sides of the entrance in one-inch thick acrylic letters.

"In the end, the client reports that the results go far beyond his expectations," concludes Ruscio. *"The national expansion is well underway, with several offers for prime locations in prime shopping centers and certain stores even surpassing the sales figures of their goliath competitor, Spring. Considering the cost vs. the results, which seem to indicate a much higher amount of money being spent in the store, the design proves that it is possible to 'design with less' and achieve great results!"*

Branded merchandise is displayed on white shelving units.

Red is everywhere, accented with white shelving and black-and-white image graphics.

DESIGN
Ruscio Studio, Montréal, QC, Canada

STORE SIZE
167 m2 (1,800 sq. ft.)

PHOTOGRAPHER
Leeza Studio, Montreal, QC, Canada

Selected
Friis Shopping Center, Aalborg, Denmark

Riis Retail
Kolding, Denmark

Located in the Friis shopping center in Aalborg, Denmark, this recently opened Selected shop — designed by Riis Retail — houses both men's and women's fashions within 173 m2 of space. Although the brand's concept is unisex, men and women still have their own areas within the space and the design needed to clearly define these areas to allow both sexes to move about the shop in his or her comfort zone. Everyone always needs to be clear that they are shopping in the "right" area. That said, there is complete unity between the *femme* and *homme* sections of the store and one never doubts that the two halves are one concept — one brand.

Dividing the space into the two sections is a metal grid that creates a transparent wall. Unfinished looking wooden boxes of various sizes are attached to this grid and appear to float in the middle of the store. The boxes serve as display cabinets and furniture and hold both hanging merchandise and folded stock. Overhead another metal grid supports light fixtures and connects the two sides of the shop.

With a limited materials list of pine, raw steel and concrete — used in their purest form — the designers have created a wide array of detail within the theme of "urban lifestyle." Everywhere one looks there is an incredible variety of fixtures, furnishings and props, but this variety stays within the boundaries of the urban theme and an overall cohesive look is achieved.

"Urban" becomes "industrial" with the concrete flooring underfoot and the network of grey duct work on the ceiling. Suggested on the wall behind the cash/wrap are the sort of huge industrial fans found in a factory or warehouse.

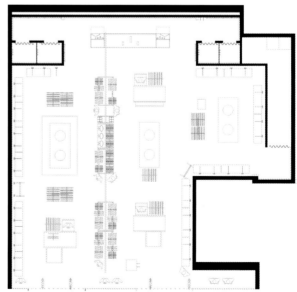

ABOVE AND OPPOSITE: The rough-hewn "boxes" that divide the *femme* and *homme* sides of the shop.
ABOVE BELOW: Details of the fixtures and cases.

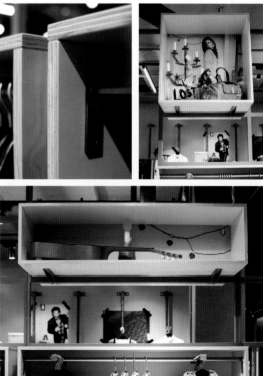

No two visual presentations are the alike, but within the variety there is still a unity of urban style and mood. Colors are neutral and materials are limited to wood, raw steel and concrete.

ABOVE RIGHT AND TOP: The cash/wrap, itself a plain wood box, is backed by industrial-looking graphics.
ABOVE LEFT: The ceiling adds to the industrial/urban look with its network of ducts and steel. **BELOW:** Everywhere one looks, there are interesting and diverse details that provide variety and interest to the small space.

DESIGN
Riis Retail A/S, Kolding, Denmark
Dennis Madsen, Jacob Guldmann

STORE SIZE
173 m2 (1,862 sq. ft.)

TECHNICAL ASSISTANT
Marianne Plet

PRODUCT DEVELOPMENT
Torben Vad Nissen

PRODUCT MANAGERS
Lasse Thomsen, Danni Sejrup

PHOTOGRAPHER
Jens Peter Engedal

La Martina

In Store Diseño

Santiago

La Martina is an Argentinean brand that embraces the polo lifestyle, selling clothing and equipment for the polo field itself, as well as sportswear and accessories that reflect the game and the lifestyle.

The brand first entered the Chilean market as a shop-within-a-shop in Falabella, the country's leading department store. Recently La Martina has expanded into stand-alone, shops of their own from which they hope to build a more up-market and influential customer base — and compete head on with Polo Ralph Lauren. Shown here is a new store in the Alto Las Condes Shopping Center, the brand's second stand-alone location.

The assignment to In Store Diseño, the shop's designers, was to deliver a store that was similar to the first location (also designed by In Store Diseño), but refined to improve the atmosphere and perfect the brand image. The new design includes many of the same elements as the first, but is realized in a larger space with increased finesse. Consistency, however,

ABOVE: The first room customers enter has dark wood and a checkerboard floor and displays the products actually used on the polo field.
BELOW: The second room displays color-coordinated merchandise on white-painted shelving.

Vital to the ambiance of the store are all the little touches that reflect the sport of polo and the brand's projected lifestyle, while adding a home-like atmosphere.

DESIGN
2011, Amalia Pérez, In Store Diseño, Santiago, Chile
La Martina Team, Buenos Aires, Argentina

STORE SIZE
180 m2 (1,937.5 sq. ft.)

FIXTURES
La Martina, In Store Diseño

LIGHTING
In Store Diseño

PHOTOGRAPHY
In Store Diseño

is very important to La Martina, and the two locations need to work together to develop a strong brand image which customers will remember — vital to a new brand entering the market.

The store is divided into three rooms. The first, in brown wood and black-and-white checkerboard flooring, sells sports equipment and apparel with the insignias of various polo clubs. The next two rooms are designed in white-painted wood with warm wood flooring. The second sells sportswear and the third displays the brand's leather products, accessories and women's clothing.

As customers enter the store, the entire space — all three rooms — can be seen in a glance, as can the cash/wrap, which is the focal point of the store and located at the end of the central aisle.

Creating a home-like atmosphere was important to La Marina and lighting an integral component in achieving the desired results. Also essential to the all-important atmosphere of the store are the little touches that reflect the sport of polo and project the brand's lifestyle. Amalia Perez from In Store Diseño explains, *"The most challenging part of this assignment was to find all the visual merchandising props that help create the store's ambience. The old leather bags, the silver cups, the natural fiber carpets, the leather seats and sofas, among others, were the difficult to find, yet fun to search out in the city's antique markets."*

EKA

Future Research Design Company
Bangalore, India

EKA is a Sanskrit word meaning "one" or "singular" — a fitting name for this Bangalore shop that sells Indian arts and crafts to higher income, urban customers looking for unique, hand-crafted products. Recently, due to a word-of-mouth increase in popularity, the retailer needed to relocate to a larger space, and asked Future Research Design Company (FRDC) of Bangalore to design of a new ground-floor, 186 m2 store.

The directive from the client was straightforward: the product was the star, the real hero of the design. The resulting plan, including visual merchandising, had to embrace traditional Indian sensibilities and allow each product to be seen, felt and absorbed within an ambience that was bold, yet secondary to the product. Adding to the challenge was the fact that the products defy traditional retail categories and are ever changing. The space had to allow for the product to evolve.

Sanjay Agarwal, founder and Director of FRDC states, *"The design language has been toned down to clean and minimal lines, earth tones and neutral backgrounds. An attempt has been made to create a cozy and comfortable, yet up-market image without getting into the 'retail' look as seen in malls and stores throughout the country today."*

The layout of the store is clean and functional without being forced, and goes hand-in-hand with the visual display to allow organic and natural circulation. Customers are invited to take their time and engage with the merchandise — taking advantage of the many focal points within the store.

A slat-wall shelving system has been incorporated to avoid a "hardware" look and fixtures are made of materials such as wood, steel and glass to create a natural look. The use of eco-friendly materials, finishes, paints and techniques are in keeping with the image of the store.

A blend of warm and natural light "models" the merchandise, presenting it to its best advantage and emphasizing its sculptural qualities.

Three huge frames serve as points of focus within the space and establish a sense of scale.

ABOVE: The most striking feature of the interior design is a bold, two-toned, striped floor that provides a strong base, or stage, for the products without overpowering them. **RIGHT:** Graphics and signage help to communicate the EKA story, but it's the merchandise that provides the full narrative.

DESIGN
Future Research Design Company,
Bangalore, India

STORE SIZE
186 m2 (2,002 sq. ft.)

FIXTURES
Disha Retail, Bangalore, India

LIGHTING
Plus Light, Mumbai, India

PUMA Black
New York

Bergmeyer Associates, Inc.
Boston

When Puma took over a raw space, most recently used as a gallery, in New York City's Meatpacking District, they hired Bergmeyer to create a space that would reflect an idea that's concisely stated on the PUMA website, "Puma starts in sports and ends in fashion." The assignment was to express the brand, reinforce the sub-brands on offer in the new store, create a tie to sports and reference the Meatpacking District.

The Meatpacking District, on West 14th Street, was, as its name implies, once bustling with large, wholesale meatpackers. The area still bustles, but over the last decade or two has transformed into a major fashion neighborhood. Puma's new neighbors include Alexander McQueen, Ten Thousand Things, Stella McCartney, Jeffrey and La Perla. *"This is the right location for this store,"* said Tony Bertone, Vice President of Creative Design for PUMA, *"It's at the corner of the 'It' neighborhood in fashion and it takes PUMA into a new context."*

Showcased in the new store are premier Puma sub-brands such as Neil Barrett–designed 96 Hours, Nuala by Christy Turlington, Mihara by Japanese designer Mihara Yasuhira, the vintage-inspired

ABOVE AND BELOW RIGHT: At the rear of the store merchandise is displayed on shelving suggestive of a grandstand, a nod to PUMA's ties to sports.
BELOW LEFT: A freestanding black bench is modelled after the brand's form stripe.

One wall is a graphic screen showing continuous images of ad campaigns for lines sold at the store. On the opposite wall logos for the collections are portrayed in large abstracted gray graphic patterns.

Rudolf Dassler line with Dutch designer Alexander van Slobbe, and the Philippe Starck collection of footwear. Most of the apparel and footwear retails for about $100 to $300 and the offerings are skewed to a slightly older customer than typical for PUMA. Also of note, the store carries no products from the mainstream Puma brand.

Joseph Nevin, Senior Principal at Bergmeyer says, *"We created a venue in which PUMA could exhibit its premier sub-brands and collaborative projects — a store that would act as a laboratory or incubator for the brand to experiment with new ideas and infuse the PUMA personality with the design sensibility of experts from various industries. The design team created a setting that would directly connect with an upscale consumer."*

When consumers think of PUMA, two distinctive logos come to mind: the jumping cat and the form stripe found on the side of a Puma shoe. While previous concept stores have looked to the jumping cat for design inspiration, the PUMA Black Store takes its lead from the brand's signature form stripe. It was the motivation behind the curved walls, the curved slots in the ceiling, and the freestanding black bench.

On the front door an unobtrusive PUMA logo with its accompanying panther are in black instead of the traditional red — further setting the store apart from other Puma locations.

"Intended to highlight the unique aspects of a multitude of collections in an inclusive space," explains Nevin, *"the store has a black interior that provides a neutral backdrop to focus consumers' attention onto the designs of each product range. The fixtures in the store are inspired by sport and placed strategically so that all brands can intersect and interact in a unique way."*

The stores ties to sports and its Meatpacking location are expressed in unique and understated ways — tubular metal perimeter and floor fixtures on wheels were fabricated by a Boston-based bicycle shop; and rock climbers' carabiners attached with nylon straps to the original structure play on both sport and hanging meat.

With this store, brand, store location and product unite to invite consumers to look at a familiar brand from a different angle.

The design is open and uncluttered, very little touches the floor.

DESIGN
Bergmeyer Associates, Inc., Boston, MA

CLIENT DESIGNER
Antonio Bertone, Chief Marketing Officer for PUMA

STORE SIZE
186 m2 (2,000 sq. ft.)

FIXTURES
Independent Fabrication, Newmarket, NH

LIGHTING
Standard Electric

PHOTOGRAPHY
Chun Y Lai

Floor fixtures on wheels were fabricated by a bicycle shop and the rock climbers' carabiners represent both sports and the neighborhood's meatpacking past.

Tess & Carlos
Newton Centre, Massachusetts

Bergmeyer Associates, Inc.
Boston

The owners of Tess & Carlos, a high-end women's apparel, shoe and accessory boutique, recently wanted to further develop their retail operation — and their brand — by expanding Carlos, the shoe and accessory component of the store and opening a small restaurant next door to the boutique. While the expansion of Carlos provided much needed showroom space for the retail operation, the new, adjacent restaurant, Pava, positions Tess & Carlos as a complete lifestyle brand by adding fine dining to the customers' options.

Bergmeyer Associates, in collaboration with the owners Tess Enright and Carlos Pava, created a bright, clean, gallery-like setting which unites three separate buildings and two unlikely functions into one, seamless brand experience.

Because the structural columns and the floor levels of the three original spaces were not aligned, the design team developed additive and subtractive volumes and planes to conceal oddly-placed beams, ductwork and roof drains. The resulting structures and shapes give a distinctive positive/negative interplay to the space. Ramping the floors at a low pitch allows the sidewalk to seamlessly flow into the store, bringing the retailer into compliance with accessibility regulations and mediating between the existing floor levels.

The central display feature in the boutique artfully hides a secondary purpose — the frosted glass display shelves can be removed for cleanout access to Pava's lower-level kitchen exhaust hoods.

Through the extensive use of glass and a shared materials palette of raw plaster, polished concrete, stainless steel and ebonized mahogany, an environment is created in which boutique, restaurant — and the stretch of sidewalk out front — act as one. The minimalist gallery setting provides a quiet, sculpture backdrop for the beautifully designed and crafted merchandise while inviting customers to "see and be seen."

DESIGN
Bergmeyer Associates, Inc.
Boston, MA

STORE SIZE
186 m2 (2,000 sq. ft.)

PHOTOGRAPHY
Greg Premru

The design seeks to make the elegant lifestyle of Tess & Carlos inviting and accessible — visually and physically — through the use of glass and a spatial orientation to the public street in front of the building.

Utopia Records

Sydney

Eileen Kamp

Sydney

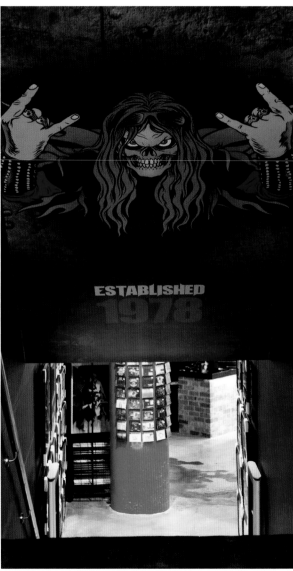

Utopia Records, established in 1978, is an institution for metal music in Sydney, selling new and used CDs, vinyl records, DVDs (including a fast-growing horror range), collectables and memorabilia from around the world, books and a small range of fashion and accessories. The store's core customers are 25–55 year old men looking for metal and classic rock, but there's also a growing teen market searching for vinyl records.

Recently new owners made the decision to relocate from just outside Sydney's center back to the heart of city where Utopia was founded. A brave move as it meant going from 750 m2 of space to a mere 189.5 m2. The owners' instruction to the design firm Eileen Kamp were stark and simple: "Design a shop that fits all this stuff into a much smaller space… and oh, it's a basement!"

"The amount of stock held in the previous space was mindboggling," says Eileen Kamp. *"The main challenge was to work through all the product categories and decide what was to stay and what was to go. Another big challenge was the basement location – how could we draw attention to the store and encourage people to come down from off the street? We had restricted ability to alter the façade of the building."*

The new space had been an old and outdated camping store, complete with baby-blue walls, low ceiling tiles and worn nylon carpet. Kamp states, *"To add to this eye sore, the space is an awkward shape with three large structural columns interspersed at odd locations throughout… however, we saw the potential.*

"While it was imperative to approach the design of

FAR LEFT: Entry foyer with illuminated Utopia logo.
LEFT: Utopias ominous "Metal Man" welcomes customers with double devil horns as they descend the stairs into the main retail area.

The sales counter — made from recycled bricks with blackened steel top — anchors the space and serves as a multi-functional workstation

the new space with a strict hand, to create a sense of order and functionality," Kamp continues, "it was extremely important to the owners and staff to avoid creating a 'cookie cutter' music store environment. The owner's instruction to create a safe and inspiring space for like-minded people had to be held in high regard at all times."

The first step, after ripping out the carpet and ceiling tiles and painting the walls almost black, was to deal with the foyer, the only part of the store on street level and visible from the street. Floor, ceiling and walls were blacked out and one wall was covered with large album covers as a backdrop to the illuminated logo. To involve the staff, each was invited to choose his or her favorite album cover for the wall. Another section of the foyer was designed to involve

customers and fitted with corkboards and plinths to allow them to hang street press and posters.

"This zone was an immediate success," says Kamp. "Customers can freely pin up gig posters advertising the local metal scene and the album wall has become an attraction in itself. Customers and even passing tourists will stop to have their photograph taken with the feature wall."

Down in the basement the space was gutted. Removal of the ceiling tiles visually heightened the space and exposed an array of plumbing, service pipes, a/c ducts and rusty-looking cement slabs. All perfect backdrops for Utopia's image. Suspended steel cable trays were introduced to house directional metal halides and the stage can lights featured above the sales counter.

Under the carpeting the designers found a rough-textured cement floor, also perfect for the metal music scene. This was sanded and sealed just enough to create a safe surface, while retaining its unique look.

In order to tame the unusual shape of the space and create an easy shopping environment, departments were placed in clearly-defined zones. The fashion zone, which could be treated with the most "theatrics," was placed in the rear of the space to visually draw customers through the entire store. Adding warmth to both the fashion zone and the sales counter are recycled bricks. Located at opposite ends of the space, the bricks serve to unify the odd-shaped space.

To contrast with the grungy, textured look of the shell, fixture units were designed in raw black metal finish with simple, sleek lines. Floor units are based on a modular system with interchangeable bases and tops. This all-important flexibility was key to fitting

the vast amount of stock into such a small space. Kamps explains, *"CD and DVD units were mathematically designed to hold as many discs as possible on the floor. Wall fixtures are also flexible enough to rotate stock throughout the store. For example, a vinyl merchandising shelf can become a shoe display or a platform to display a range of collectable character toys. Investment in the design and production of these units, within an otherwise conservative budget, allowed for the dramatic downsize of the store.*

"Overall, the response has been tremendous," Kamp concludes. *"Staff and customers cannot believe that such a significant downsize in retail space can hold everything they need. Nothing is missed! As for the original request for a safe, inspiring place for like minded people? The customer feedback has been extremely positive. It's a familiar yet stimulating, non-pretentious den for Utopias old time and new wave customers."*

DESIGN
Eileen Kamp, Sydney, Australia
STORE SIZE
189.5 m2 (2,040 sq. ft.)
FIXTURES
Interspace, Sydney, Australia
CONSTRUCTION
Double D Building Pty Ltd, Sydney, Australia
PHOTOGRAPHER
Sonsoles Fueyo Hidalgo

ABOVE LEFT: The merchandising units in the CD/DVD zone have been designed as a flexible modular system. The timber cupboards can be removed, and the tops of the units can be interchanged to accommodate changes in stock levels between DVDs and CDs. **TOP RIGHT:** The clean lines of the floor units were designed to contrast with the heavily textured shell of the store and create a sense of order within the space.
ABOVE RIGHT: Raw blackened steel was used in the construction of the fixtures. All the marks that accumulated on the steel during production remain visible, lending a nice quality to the pieces.

Dalú

Florida Center Mall, Santiago, Chile

Droguett A&A Ltda

Santiago, Chile

The polished stainless steel window frames of the main facade and the brand logo flowers of the doors are clearly noticed from the hallway. Purple ceiling lights are a main design feature of the interior.

When first created as a new brand by Empresas Bercovich, Dalú was relegated to its own space within Privilege stores. Dalú targeted an audience of younger women with a desire for clothing and accessories outside the parameters of standard fashion trends.

Within a short period of time, Dalú captured a rapidly expanding clientele and Empresas Bercovich concluded the Dalú brand needed its own retail store space in the Chilean market. Freddy Droguett, of A&A Ltda., was chosen for that process. *"Our goal was to develop a unique store image completely opposite from the Privilege stores. Also, it had to be a space readily suited to large seasonable changes and easily adaptable to significant renovation,"* says Droguett.

That unique store personality evolved by utilizing purple ceiling lighting cascading through a polished steel grid. Every fixture and display rack is made of mirror-polished stainless steel reflecting the purple cast throughout the store. The high gloss floor also reflects the purple color, while ceiling lighting gives a feeling of openness in a futuristic surrounding. Merchandise, however, is illuminated by spotlights and high-hats to maintain merchandise color integrity. A delightful richness is achieved using matte black vinyl, wave-textured gray wall covering, black painted glass, and mural photographs for back surfaces of the clothing displays. The Dalú brand logo flowers are repeated on entry doors, gray wall panels, and prominently featured on the cashier counter island.

Summing up, Droguett says, *"We needed to think locally, creating an image for a local store chain, and yet, keep looking with a vision of international expansion for this rapidly growing brand. We have produced the look of trendy sophistication."* Dalú will leap borders effortlessly.

ABOVE: View from the front of the store. **BELOW:** View from the back to the front. Cozy chairs behind the cashier counter face the dressing room entrance for comfortable consultations.

ABOVE LEFT: Located at the center of the space is the cashier counter with four custom light fixtures suspended above it made of muslin strips hand-wound on wire spheres. **ABOVE RIGHT:** On both sides of the store, the clothing exhibition areas have giant photos of spring trees. Note the wash of purple-tinted light spilling down the wall. Purple filters cover light tubes within the white light box, filling it with the bold hue that radiates in broad bands of color between the narrow, highly-polished steel strips. Look closely to see the vertical baffles between each fixture. **BELOW:** An extensive accessories collection including purses, belts, jewelry, etc., is highlighted in several specialized wall displays and table fixtures throughout the space.

DESIGN
Droguett A&A ltda, Santiago, Chile

SPACE
190 m2 (2,045 sq. ft.)

ARCHITECT, DIRECTOR
Freddy Droguett H.

ARCHITECT, PROJECT DESIGNER
Tomás González

GENERAL CONTRACTOR
Andres Link, Constructora LNK

CEO
Arturo Bercovich

GENERAL MANAGER
Alex Bercovich

PHOTOGRAPHER
Marcos Mendizábal

ABOVE LEFT: Dressing rooms are comfortably spacious so patrons can change and then step out into the wide, elegant viewing area complete with a giant wall mirror to check out their selected outfits. All metal finishes, as they are throughout the store, are mirror-polished; black velvet curtains complement the grey walls.
ABOVE RIGHT: Tables and wall displays are spotlighted with clear light to emphasize the items shown.

Arenal2
Madrid

MARKETING-JAZZ
Madrid

The challenge for Carlos Aires and MARKETING-JAZZ was to create a new identity for Arenal2 pharmacy and to provide a more modern, updated appearance without touching the floors, ceiling or lighting. And, he had to do all this in two months.

Arenal2, founded in 1855, is one of Madrid's oldest pharmacies and one of Spain's most respected. Throughout its long history the company has maintained a reputation for trustworthiness and fair prices. Today, its philosophy continues to compel it to provide expert prescription service and offer inexpensive, yet chic cosmetics and personal-care products.

MARKETING JAZZ was charged with improving the buying experience and designing the environment to more clearly communicate the brand philosophy — all *without* making structural changes

or even closing the pharmacy during renovation.

What the designers *did* do within this limited directive was to reorganize the space and imagine a new way of presenting the product. Aires states, *"Redesigning means taking maximum advantage of existing resources. We panelled the furniture to create a new visual merchandising style that was appropriate for the different product categories: Skincare, First Aid, Children, Oral, Natural Medicine, OTC. The customer will now find pallets, cardboard boxes, employee portraits, blackboards with messages, decorative vinyl and background music. The modern touch was provided by the design of a counter in the form of a cross for the main cash register and prescription medicines area."*

That cross (the version with arms of equal length), figures prominently in the redesign. Not only does

ABOVE: The space was renovated without structural changes or changes to the floor or ceiling. One unique addition, however, are the lighting sources installed in the pallets that hold the cardboard boxes. **OPPOSITE:** The main cash register/pharmacy counter is in the shape of a cross.

the cash register and prescription counter form a cross, but the symbol appears on the glass of an interior display case and in the pharmacy's four display windows.

Aires explains, *"The idea came from considering how to clearly transmit the selection of products available at the Arenal2 pharmacy. We focused on three elements: The cross, our product and the lighting."*

The windows are filled with products organized by category, color and shape, all arranged around an empty space in the shape of a cross outlined in LEDs.

Other important additions to the store are the employee photos that appear at important focal

points, creatively communicating the brand's dedication to personal service. Also adding a personal touch as well as providing pricing and prescription information are the blackboards that are attached to almost every available surface.

Without major, or expensive, structural changes MARKETING-JAZZ has brought a pharmacy with a long history into the 21st century while retaining the trust the brand had long established between itself and its customers. As Aires succinctly sums it up, *"a traditional soul with a modern and smart approach."*

ABOVE: Another view of the central cross-shaped counter. **BELOW:** Handwritten messages appear everywhere one looks and, along with large photos of friendly employees, add a personal touch to the space.

DESIGN
MARKETING-JAZZ, Madrid

STORE SIZE
200 m2 (2,153 sq. ft.)

CREATIVE DIRECTOR AND FURNITURE DESIGN
Carlos Aires

SKETCHES AND ILLUSTRATIONS
Elena de Andrés

3D DESIGN
Alejandro Andreu

DELINEATION
Juan José López Cámara

VISUAL MERCHANDISING
**Carlos Aires, Itziar Esteban Infantes de Borja,
Silvia Bellisco**

WINDOW ASSEMBLY
Itziar Esteban Infantes de Borja

PHOTOGRAPHER
**Luis Sánchez de Pedro Aires,
Airesphotostudio**

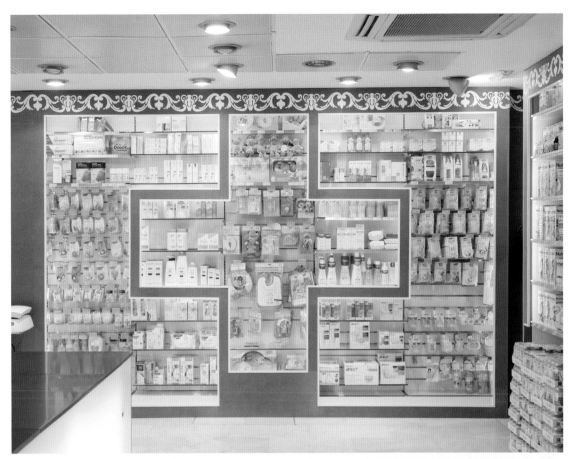

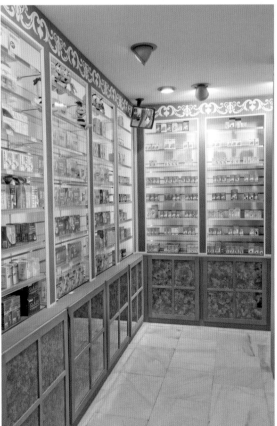

TOP: One on the display cases incorporates a cross. **ABOVE RIGHT:** Spotlights highlight the neatly arranged products. **ABOVE LEFT:** The cross also appears in the pharmacy's display windows.

MEXX

Rhein Center Koln, Cologne, Germany

MEXX Creative Team
Umdasch *Amstetten, Austria*

ABOVE: The "X" marks the entrance doors. **BELOW:** Details of the store include a "hand" to hold a featured bag and a branding "globe."

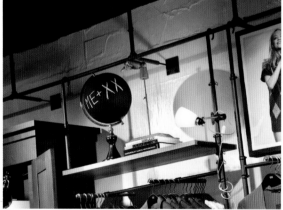

DESIGN
MEXX Creative Team
Store Consult by Umdasch, Amstetten, Austria

STORE SIZE
200 m2 (2,153 sq. ft.)

SHOP FITTING
Jonas

PHOTOGRAPHY
Fotoquelle Mexx/Philippi

"Everything is New" is the motto for the fashion label MEXX, and the new look is evident in the comprehensive brand relaunch of the company and in the new retail setting revealed here in Cologne. The 200 m2 shop was designed with the cooperative efforts of the MEXX creative team working very closely with the Shop Consult of Umdasch. The new concept effects a "Metropolitan Casual Lifestyle."

According to the MEXX CEO, Thomas Grote, *"MEXX is inspired by big-city life and precisely that is what you will see and feel in our new stores."* Authenticity and individualism are the characteristics of the design and future stores — based on this concept — will still tell their own stories. Underlining the *"authenticity of this lifestyle impression"* are the materials, the graffiti, and the themes and props that suggest travel — on the go — movement.

The rough textured, off-white walls, herringbone patterned fumed oak floors, antique-looking wall coverings and the black metal pipe display system are all so urban — so much the city. The black painted ceiling camouflages a multitude of wires and pipes and a white floating panel hangs down over the central display area. The lighting that highlights the featured garments on the mannequins below is contained within this focal structure.

Seen from the mall, the shopfront consists of two giant floor-to-ceiling, glass-enclosed display windows featuring abstract and headless mannequins. They are backed up by gigantic graphic panels showing the latest in MEXX apparel. Overscaled, as well, are the wood paneled doors that stand open and welcoming. The fumed oak wood finish is carried over onto the wood floors inside.

Charcoal gray armoires stand along some of the walls showcasing fashion or color stories while the natural wood shelves on the black pipe fitting system carries folded stock, hung garments, dressed forms and fun props. The display system was created by the Umdasch firm using water pipes that can be suspended from the ceiling and clamps for the adjustable shelf supports or moveable hang rods. According to the designers, *"the lighting echoes the main themes consistently and bathes the store in a warm soft ambience."*

(METROPOLITAN CASUAL) MeT'Rə-PɪLɪTᴀᴺ bɪ'KᴀᴢᴜᴇL
TYPICAL MEXX STYLE INSPIRED BY METROPOLITAN CITIES
→ ADDING XX TO YOUR LIFE → ME + XX _0.1 ME + S¬XX _0.2 ME +
RELAXXED, _0.3 ME + EXXPRESSIVE → DESIGNED TO EXXCITE. MEXX

Privilege

Plaza Vespucio Mall, Santiago, Chile

Droguett A&A Ltda

Santiago, Chile

Large window frames made of dark wood, a grid of silver circles, and the polished steel "PG" logo all serve to attract passersby in the mall.

In operation for almost 100 years, Privilege is one of the most respected retailers of women's apparel in Chile, and operates more than 15 stores throughout the country. In its long history, the company has always been forward thinking in the development of its image, and has continually updated its brand.

That's why the retailer recently took advantage of a new store it had planned for the Plaza Vespucio Mall to seek out new ideas for its image. The retailer held an architecture competition to select a designer for the new space. The challenge of the contest was to reinforce the brand's personality and its differentiating attributes while creating a new image that would appeal to a younger, more sophisticated target market than the older stores.

Freddy Droguett and his firm Droguett A&A of Santiago, who had worked previously with Privilege, won the contest, and the winning design, in addition to the Plaza Vespucio store, will be applied to future store openings and refurbishings.

Droguett describes the situation, *"Privilege is one of our oldest clients and we've been working together for almost ten years. For that reason, to work on an image-changing design wasn't an easy task for us. We needed, as a design team, a new approach and a new way of working."*

Two important aspects of the assignment were to, first, design and introduce a new "PG" logo, and second, to create a decorative element within the store that would be recognized by consumers as unique to Privilege. Droguett states. *"To achieve these tasks we created the circle-matrix grid that is applied on the main doors, and the cubic structure located in the middle of the store. The grid will also be used as a marketing element."*

Other tasks made explicit by the retailer were to increase the capacity of the displays and to create a display area for a product line new to the retailer — jeans.

The overall color palette of the new design is

A centrally-located visual display element divides the store and can be seen from the mall hallway. Color-changing RGB LED wall-washer spotlights bath the display's grid in changing colors. The floor incorporates two coverings: a middle beige, marble-like porcelain tile is used over most of the space while, at the center, dark wood leads from the entrance, under the central display element and back to the cash/wrap.

darker than the older stores and completely changes the ambience of the space. What were mainly white walls and ceilings with light brown woods is now darker — walls, wood coverings and floors. The main finishings are dark wood and dark paint, polished stainless steel fixturing and aged, silver foil coverings.

The lighting in the new space is also very different. Instead of the high ambient light with no particular accents of the old stores, the ambient light is now quite low with theater-style spotlights providing accent lighting in every display area.

"Although they have long held a position as an important market actor, Privilege needed to be a trend definer, a brand which was followed by others," states Droguett. *"We wanted to create a leading image, with a strong and unique brand character."*

They certainly succeeded.

The overall dark and neutral hues of the store help to create a sophisticated interior.

The wall behind the dress display is covered with aged silver foil that acts as a neutral backdrop for the merchandise and becomes a feature of the store that customers identify with the brand.

DESIGN
Droguett A&A ltda, Santiago, Chile

STORE SIZE
200 m2 (2,153 sq. ft.)

ARCHITECT, DIRECTOR
Freddy Droguett H.

ARCHITECT, PROJECT DESIGNER
Roberto Pertuz D.

GENERAL CONTRACTOR
Alex Zóffoli, Constructora Zoff

STORE CEO
Arturo Bercovich

STORE GENERAL MANAGER
Alex Bercovich

PHOTOGRAPHER
Marcos Mendizábal

California Academy of Sciences Retail Stores

Golden Gate Park, San Francisco

BALDAUF CATTON VON ECKARTSBERG Architects

San Francisco

BALDAUF CATTON VON ECKARTSBERG Architects were tasked with the design of the three retail spaces located within Renzo Piano's new California Academy of Sciences building. The building houses research facilities, the Steinhart Aquarium, Morrison Planetarium and the Kimball Natural History Museum. *"The stores,"* says Hans Baldauf of BCV, *"are envisioned as integral to the experience of the Academy, allowing visitors to 'take a piece of the academy home.' The design for each store seeks to extend themes raised in the design of the larger building, including the building's role within the environment and ecosystem of Golden Gate Park, and make the history of the Academy integral to the designs."*

The three retail spaces are Academy Store (202 m2) located in the main entrance and carrying the broadest range of products; Lab Junior (123.5 m2) located adjacent to the Planetarium and the children's education area and focused on youth-related products; and the tiny Swamp Store (31 m2) located on the mezzanine level of the Steinhart Aquarium and offering Aquarium-related products. *"Each separate store,"* says Baldauf, *"has to reflect the character of the museum, and its research, specimens and its exhibits – whose mission is to 'explore, explain and protect the natural world.'"*

The casework for all three stores is inspired by the wood paneling traditionally found in natural history libraries. Classic library shelving systems have been reinterpreted as systems of boxes with varying widths and depths creating a Mondrian-like pattern. The wood in the shelving is from 17 different tree species that grow in Golden Gate Park and were locally sourced. *"It is our hope that the visitor will connect the beautiful wood casework with the great urban forest on which the new building sits,"* says Baldauf.

Each store features a unique central light fixture which gives it a distinct character. In the Academy Store the central light fixture takes the form of a great, curved blue-gum vault, furthering the "wood story" of the store.

The architects chose a family of giraffe mounts and a whale skeleton to frame the Lab Junior store and integrate it into the museum. This store is envisioned as an interactive space with a large "lab table" composed of wood boxes and specimen vitrines defining the center of the store. Here children can use microscopes and other items that they are then able to purchase — "taking home" the museum experience. The space is defined by a sculptural light armature inspired by the great whale skeleton found outside the store. Designed in collaboration with a noted wood boat builder, this armature consists of ten complex steamed frames of ribs which hold a wooden hull supporting both up and down lighting. "The architects hope that children (and adults) will enjoy the inspiration that we took from nature," says Baldauf. The floor around the lab table features painted tiles that were located in the museum's original aquarium. The upper register of casework features historic lab instruments, specimen jars, and other scientific tools.

The rear of the store is anchored by an original library table celebrating the research that is at the core of the Academy. Throughout the upper level of casework, artifacts from the museum's collections are displayed, making emphatic the connection between the store and surrounding institution.

All three stores employ sustainable practices as much as possible, patterned after the museum's LEED platinum certification. The HVAC system ties into the base building, which is naturally ventilated, and the vast majority of the light fixtures used in the stores are energy efficient metal halide or LED.

"Each retail store has been created to be unique and to support a common aesthetic that ties them to the surrounding building and environment. They have been designed to celebrate the future while acknowledging the importance of the past," concludes Baldauf.

The Swamp Store celebrates the fusion of old and new. The exterior of the store is clad in a mixture of tiles salvaged from the original building and new recycled glass tiles. Two sets of original bronze doors were utilized, one carefully restored and converted into the sliding doors, while the other set provided the bronze for the tiny turtles and fish that grace the circular metal chandelier and the sliding doors — some stylized fish acting as door handles. The upper register of casework in this store exhibits aquarium collection tools, specimens, and photographs of past exhibits and of the original aquarium.

DESIGN
BALDAUF CATTON VON ECKARTSBERG Architects
San Francisco, CA

STORE SIZES
Academy Store: **202 m2** (2,173 sq. ft.)
Lab Junior: **123.5 m2** (1,330 sq. ft.)
Swamp Store: **31.3 m2** (337 sq. ft.)

LIGHTING
Revolver Design, Berkeley, CA

CONTRACTOR
Webcor Builders, San Francisco CA

WHALE LIGHT FIXTURE
Soren Hansen's Woodcraft, Alameda CA

WALRUS REPRODUCTION AND SWAMP TILE BASE
Edge Innovations, Alameda, CA

SIGNAGE
Martinelli Environmental Graphics, San Francisco, CA

MILLWORK
Plant Architectural Woodwork, San Francisco, CA

WOOD VENEER
Arborica, Petaluma, CA;
Exotic Hardwoods and Veneers, Oakland, CA

PHOTOGRAPHERS
Sharon Risedorph Photography,
Rien van Rijthoven Architecture Photography

PUMA

Paris

Plajer & Franz Studio
Berlin

Treating the product as a hero the store design not only enhances the display of PUMA'S performance and lifestyle articles but intentionally works as a product category navigation.

Located on Boulevard de Sébastopol between the famous Forum de Halles and the Centre Pompidou, PUMA'S Parisian flagship recently reopened following a complete renovation. The new concept was developed by Plajer & Franz Studio and Ales Kernjak, global store concept manager for PUMA retail.

The goal of the designers, as described by Werner Franz of Plajer & Franz Studio, *"was to bring joy back into the retail environment while aiming for a sustainable and innovative retail design."* The new store incorporates creative input from the Parisian artists' collective 9th Concept, as well as cutting-edge technology developed by GBH Design Limited and Spies & Assassins to facilitate interactive customer engagement.

PUMA occupies two floors of a corner building and covers slightly more than 200 m2 of space. On offer is a broad range of footwear, apparel and accessories, including PUMA'S black label, which features the brand's collaborations with Hussein Chalayan

TOP: Shoe-shaped window fixtures present a "shoe" to passersby on the street and serve as shelving inside the store.
ABOVE LEFT: PUMA'S red, signature wall decorates the stairwell. **ABOVE RIGHT:** In the fitting rooms the "peepshow" boxes provide customers one of many opportunities to interact with the brand.

and Alexander McQueen. Footwear, however, is still at PUMA'S core and is given the most attention and the highest priority in presentation and visibility.

In the upper windows, displays in the iconic shape of a PUMA Suede shoe function as both window display and fixture. The shoe, seen in color from the street, supports shelving inside the store.

"Generally customer interaction is written in big letters at PUMA and therefore an important aspect of the store design, including the integration of the latest communication channels," says Ales Kernjak.

iPads are not only scattered around the shop attached to display tables, but are also assembled at the "PUMA joy pad"— a huge iPad wall, framed in red transparent glass, that lets customers interact with PUMA using specially-developed "apps." In the future this will be extended to live streaming connections to other PUMA stores.

Referencing the past, while having some fun in the present, are the old-school telephones — "un-

DESIGN
Plajer & Franz Studio, Berlin, Germany
Ales Kernjak, global store concept manager for PUMA retail

STORE SIZES
207 m2 (2,228 sq. ft.)

PROJECT MANAGEMENT
Patricia Senft

LOCAL ARTISTS
9th Concept, Paris, France

MARKETING ACTIVITIES / "REDWORLD ELEMENTS"
GBH Design Limited, London, UK, www.gregorybonnerhale.com
creative role: branding and brand expression
Spies & Assassins, New York, NY, www.spies.ws
creative role: creative technology

LIGHTING
XAL Xenon Architectural Lighting gmbh, Indersdorf, Germany

STORE CONSTRUCTION
Dula-Werke Dustmann & Co. gmbh, Vreden, Germany

PHOTOGRAPHER
Manuel Schlüter ©PUMA ag

"Un-smart" phones and iPads relay brand messages to consumers.

smart" phones — that are placed around the space and play random messages when picked up. In the fitting rooms the idea of a colorful and joyful retail experience is expressed with special "PUMA Peepshow" boxes. These red boxes open to expose the

unexpected — be it a video clip or product presentation. Phones (both smart and un-smart) and the peepshow boxes further customer engagement with the brand.

Also adding brand appeal is a six-meter-high wall, in PUMA'S signature red, that acts as a connecting element between the floors. Built from separate and removable cubes it can be changed randomly.

PUMA'S embracement of the joyful elements of retailing in no way lessens its commitment to sustainability. The design uses ecological sound materials such as FSC certified wood and floor finishes, low-emitting paint and an efficient lighting mix to save energy consumption.

The design, PUMA'S first step in pursuit of a truly novel retail experience, will rollout in other locations and countries.

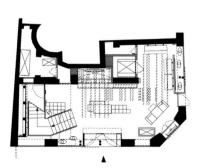

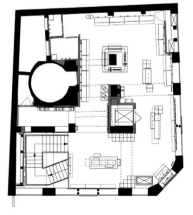

Rockford (RKF)

La Dehesa Mall, Santiago

dearQ Architecture & Design

Santiago

The Rockford Company has for some time extolled *"outdoor life within an environment that resembles nature."* Rockford, also known as RKF, specializes in casual wear and sports shoes for men and women and has established nature-themed stores throughout Chile.

In this, the company's new store in Santiago, the dearQ Architecture & Design firm under the direction of Marcela Ponce de Leon Salucci, went way beyond "resembling" nature. In this retail space the store is growing green — literally — with vegetal walls filled with native species of plants and

flowers. Ponce de Leon Salucci explains, *"This gives the ambiance a unique feature; it changes as nature changes."* Just as the merchandise within the store changes with the seasons of the year, so does the décor and ambiance change as the living plants change from one growing season to the next.

A central hallway divides the space into two areas — men's and women's. A "living room" area is located in the shoe department with green climbing walls at the rear of the space. Reached through a corridor with an abundance of greenery are the dressing rooms. As in other Rockford stores in Chile, native woods and quarried stone are used. Where in the previous shops there was a rustic and rough feel to the materials, here they are smooth and finished to contrast the texture of the growing plants. Natural Coigue wood is used to surface the shop's façade and a stainless steel decoy with the RKF logo and the Rockford name are superimposed over the rough textured panels. This same multi-level texture also appears on some of the focal walls inside the store.

Since this is a "green" store — literally and figuratively — the designers had to consider the ways and means of keeping the living elements in the design alive, healthy and blooming. That required special attention to maintaining a proper temperature in the shop, providing an automatic drip irrigation system for the plants and special lighting for both day and night.

DESIGN
dearQ Architecture & Design, Santiago, Chile

STORE SIZE
210 m2 (2,260 sq. ft.)

PRINCIPAL IN CHARGE
Marcela Ponce de Leon Salucci

CONSTRUCTION
Qualitz

VISUAL MERCHANDISING
D&I (Diseño e Imagen)

PHOTOGRAPHY
dearQ Architecture & Design

O'Neill
Amsterdam

Anderson Architects
New York

A unique, Surf Pioneering Lifestyle — inspired by company founder, Jack O'Neill — is reflected throughout the shop. The central area is a surfing "garage" setting, complete with weathered cabinets and surfing memorabilia.

O'Neill is a leading lifestyle brand with a strong appeal to the surfing community and the *"young, sport-loving mainstream."* Products range from surfboard equipment to sportswear for men and women with an emphasis on an expert blend of functionality and style.

A new O'Neill retail concept was launched in this 214 m2 shop in Amsterdam. The restyled flagship store is a pilot project that will also serve as a prototype for an international roll out of new O'Neill stores. Anderson Architects concepted the design using Jack O'Neill — the founder of the company — and his life as inspiration. Influencing the design are O'Neill's home in Santa Cruz in Northern California, his close links to nature and his passion for water sports. As executed by Umdasch, the space has been divided into "worlds."

The central area of the store is the detailed garage setting where all the surf equipment is presented. A lounge with an integrated stove invites shoppers to relax and stay awhile — or continue on to the cash/wrap that is also located here. Sports and leisure wear are shown in the casual area, while bathing fashions are on view in the active "world."

The final "world" is that of the spacious fitting

rooms located at the rear on this single-level shop.

The execution of the design concept and the shop fittings were produced by Umdasch. The Umdasch team explains, *"The shopfittings create an impression of space or divide up the different areas. Even the selection of materials matches the basic theme of the concept and reflects the unspoiled nature of the northern California region. Real wood — spruce, maritime pine and oak — black untreated metal with a transparent powdered finish, concrete and galvanized metal sheeting are all employed. Nor was the color scheme left to chance. The definition of special company colors guarantee that Jack O'Neill's house is reproduced as accurately as possible."*

Authentic use of materials and colors as well as harmonious lighting arrangements characterize the appearance of this international lifestyle brand.

ABOVE: Sports and leisure wear are shown in the casual "world."
OPPOSITE: Bathing fashions are on view in the white-raftered active "world."

DESIGN CONCEPT
Anderson Architects, New York, NY

STORE SIZE
214 m2 (2,300 sq. ft.)

DESIGN EXECUTION & SHOP FITTING
Umdasch Shop Concepts, Amstetten, Austria

PHOTOGRAPHY
Courtesy of O'Neill

COX Communications Retail Store

Gonzalez, Louisiana

Commercial Design Interiors, LLC
Ritter Maher Architects

Baton Rouge, Louisiana

A rendering and a concept drawing detail the space.

COX Communications' main service is as a cable provider. The Video Feature Wall showcases their cable product and its quality.

COX Communications is a provider of cable, phone and high-speed Internet service to homes and businesses in the company's service area. Recently the company decided to explore the use of bricks-and-mortar retail spaces to connect with their client base in a new way, and reach out to potential clients with a fresh approach to marketing.

The focus of the retail stores is the company's subscription services — with price points that range from $30 to as much as $500 a month for extensive packages — but the spaces also allow COX to expand into other markets such as mobile phones and hardware.

COX tasked Commercial Design Interiors, LLC and

Ritter Maher Architects, both of Baton Rouge, with the design of this new retail store in Gonzalez, Louisiana, a town located between Baton Rouge and New Orleans. The new design had to respond to the company's extensive target market which spans all socioeconomic markets.

Matthew Edmonds of Commercial Design Interiors states, *"The concept behind The COX Communications retail location was to create a streamlined, 'digital age' environment that would generate multiple sales and embrace their current marketing strategies. The types of forms and iconic imagery used throughout the design were to give an energetic and embracing greeting, and an invitation to make oneself comfortable and study he display items at leisure."*

Spatial and visual differentiation of functions within the space had to be clear, and product displays needed to be divided by manufacturer while still maintaining a visual connection to one another. The client requested that customer service be stationed in the back of the store to create semi-private areas for customer/representative interaction.

The recent branding development of the COX Corporation was reflected in the new store design. Corporate identity is established with custom signage and the integration of the primary brand colors in the architectural elements and the secondary colors in the custom millwork displays. Edmonds explains, *"'Space age' curves —reminiscent of current marketing — and clean, bright surfaces coordinate with inviting seating arrangements and warm wood flooring. The complementary orange ceil-* *ing canopies embrace and lead the visitor in toward the central elliptical feature, from which each functional area radiates."*

Challenges faced by the designers included an expedited schedule and a limited time frame in which to complete the design; the three-dimensional model requested by the client; and a set of interior construction documents. Ongoing coordination with the corporate standards department and executives on branding updates was also necessary.

"The main design challenge beyond this was how to combine a set of established COX corporate standards, i.e. color palette, departments, technical needs, in an innovative arena that engaged their customers and enhanced the store experience," says Edmonds."

The resulting warm and inviting atmosphere is a testament to the designers' and architects' success.

BELOW: The retail space is a community based location in which customers can have direct access for billing, service upgrades and equipment servicing. **RIGHT:** The Product Displays introduce the customer to services such as broadband and phone services.

DESIGN
Commercial Design Interiors, LLC
Baton Rouge, LA

DESIGNERS
Matthew Edmonds, Tracy Burns

ARCHITECT
Ritter Maher Architects (Scott Ritter, Amy Comeaux, Blayne McRae),
Baton Rouge, LA

STORE SIZE
215.5 m2 (2,320 sq. ft.)

CUSTOM FIXTURES
Frost Woodworks

LIGHTING
Commercial Design Interiors, LLC
Ritter Maher Architects

PHOTOGRAPHER
Matthew Edmonds

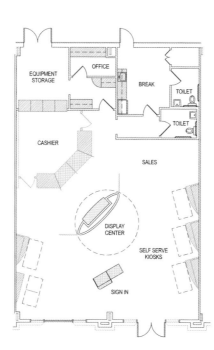

EQUIPMENT STORAGE

OFFICE

BREAK

TOILET

TOILET

CASHIER

SALES

DISPLAY CENTER

SELF SERVE KIOSKS

SIGN IN

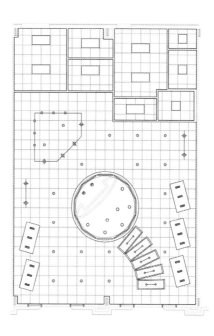

Campus by Marc O'Polo

Koenigsallee, Dusseldorf

dan Pearlman Markenarchitektur

Berlin

In a retail market where the competition is hot and heavy and boiling over with top international brand names such as Diesel, Replay, Levi's and Pepe, it was essential that Campus by Marc O'Polo make a noteworthy entrance into that market. Marc O'Polo had already established itself as a worthy brand in Europe, but Campus by Marc O'Polo, which offers casual wear and accessories for young men and women and was founded in 1972, only came into its own — as a brand — in 2006. Since then it has been opening retail stores to promote the brand concept. The concept for Campus is to display in *"an authentic, athletic, humorous, confident, sexy, unconventional way the high quality and the lives of life around campus with all its facets"* — as well as the clothing necessary for that lifestyle.

The setting for the store by dan pearlman Markenarchitektur of Berlin is unique and full of atmosphere. The authenticity of the brand is reflected in vintage surfaces made of acid treated brass, an irregular structure of plaster as well as herringbone parquet on the walls. The natural stone floors and the furniture of dark bog oak *"symbolize high quality and represent the brand."*

The corporate colors of dark blue and gold characterize the whole spatial appearance of the shop *"to create a cozy and sophisticated atmosphere."* The central lounge area of the shop is set up like a communal apartment shared by students and it is fitted with stylish vintage furnishings. Added to this, and bringing in the campus concept, are objects and bits of memorabilia of university life such as pennants, trophies and sports equipment. They become the recognizable symbols of the brand.

The 206 m2 shop invites shoppers to come in, relax and take their time to experience what one would imagine or hope campus life would be like. As the designers note, the retail concept of the brand *"quotes from the look with the atmosphere, and with the university campus lifestyle. The modern and authentic design implements the focal idea of Campus by Marc O'Polo — the feeling of freedom and independence."*

DESIGN
dan Pearlman Markenarchitektur, GmbH, Berlin, Germany

STORE SIZE
216 m2 (2,325 sq. ft.)

PHOTOGRAPHY
Renate Wildenhaim

ABOVE: The stair well and its collection of mannequins, graffiti, and suspended bike becomes a focal point of the store. The corporate colors of dark blue and gold are also present. **BELOW:** The central lounge area of the shop is set up to resemble an apartment shared by students.

4010 Telekom Shop

Cologne, Germany

parat for mutabor *Hamburg, Germany*
Dula *Dortmund, Germany*

The 4010 Telekom Shop in Cologne is much more than just a shop — it's a place where the community is invited to exchange ideas, create art, relax with friends and interact with the merchandise. And, importantly, the community in question encompasses much more than a physical location — 4010 works hard to build both virtual- and real-world exchanges of ideas. In addition to its own interactive website the company places emphasis on its social media connection points and hosts in-store workshops, exhibitions, concerts and lectures.

Included in the design are "studio" tables for customers to explore their own creativity, an Entertainment Lounge, a Gallery Wall and a Concept Room.

In a store so different from the normal telecom operation, the owners, Deutsche Telekom needed to begin the differentiation process up front, with the store's name. "4010" is the designation for the color magenta in the European color-matching system, RAL — and magenta, the company signature color, absolutely dominants the store's design. Customers are escorted into, and through, the space with a grand gesture of pink and white stripes.

For an earlier shop in Berlin, Deutsche Telekom looked to Graffiti art for inspiration, but here in Cologne, in a location surrounded by galleries, designers and fashion stores, pop art is the focus.

The challenge for the designers at Parat was to reach customers beyond the long-stranding Deutsche Telekom market and to develop and communicate a youthful and innovative image that the company did not have when first privatized in the 1990s. If design is any indication, they've certainly succeeded.

OPPOSITE: Customers are led down an entryway of pink and white stripes with all the shop's elements clearly in view. **ABOVE:** Products are displayed on trestle tables and stretched canvas as if in an artist's studio. Customers are encouraged to play with the merchandise and explore their own creativity with the art supplies spread about the tables. The lack of windows in the space was overcome by the creation of back-lit display "windows" set into the walls near the studio tables.

4010 is all about community. Everywhere one looks within the store there are areas that encourage customers to gather and relax.

The Entertainment Lounge's platform is envisioned as a "stage" for real-world community gatherings. Behind it, the Wall Gallery exhibits paintings by local artists. A 3-D TV and 3-D projector screen, Dolby Surround System, a fully-equipped DJ booth and various available lighting scenarios allow for a wide range of uses of the space.

DESIGN
parat for mutabor, Hamburg, Germany

STORE SIZE
220 m2 (2,368 sq. ft.)

SHOPFITTING
Dula, Dortmund, Germany

PHOTOGRAPHY
Dula

Clarkes Jewelers

Shreveport, Louisiana

GRID/3 International Inc.

New York

Clarkes Jewelers is owned and operated by Ginger Clarke and her son Jay Mitchell, third and fourth generation jewelers. They sell diamonds, loose and set in rings, pendants, bracelets and brooches; 18 karat and 22 karat designer jewelry and Rolex watches.

The jewelers recently moved to a new store only steps away from their previous location, but much better situated. The new store, designed by GRID/3 International, sits along a major road and is surrounded by other retailers. With the improved location the jewelers wanted to not only improve sales, but also showcase their creative brand.

Within the new store the jewelers needed separate, smaller spaces to serve various functions. Both owners needed an office. Clarke's is a private office where she can sketch ideas for marketing and jewelry designs, and Mitchell's is an "office" on the floor where, as the store's premier diamond salesperson, he can meet with clients.

Also created was a "community" space for events, trunk shows and other gatherings. Special customers are invited to this upstairs room to view higher-end merchandise. In the rear of the store a small lounge was designed for those shopping companions (usually men) who have become bored with the process and need a place to relax.

Display cases are of paramount importance when showcasing jewelry, but not all the cases in Clarkes are new. Walnut showcases that Clarke's father had commissioned in the 1960s have been updated with interior LED lighting and incorporated into the design. Since the store emphasizes diamond sales, new sit-down showcases were designed to resemble a sparkly, night sky. Designer fashion jewelry is displayed in a "360 degree" case, designed in conjunction with JMJ, that includes drawers for under stock. The sales staff has discovered that these drawers are useful selling tools as they can be pulled out to give customers a sneak preview of merchandise not on display — making them feel special and increasing sales.

As in any jewelry store, a large amount of light is required on small, delicate pieces. Adding to the challenge here was the client's desire for a layout in which the cases could be moved as interest in different categories of merchandise fluctuates. To meet this challenge, GRID/3 designed a lighting system on Con-Tech's Lux Beam track that alternates low voltage tungsten halogen and low wattage (20 watts) metal halide. This creates interest at the ceiling level, saves energy and air conditioning usage, and gives the clients the ability to relocate lighting when and if they move cases.

The owners' willingness to invest in the design and infrastructure of their store has paid off. Since opening in their new space, Clarkes Jewelers have met their new and aggressive sales goals.

RIGHT: Diamond cases were designed to resemble a night sky.
FAR RIGHT: Ginger Clarke sketches and paints on one of the walls in her office. The surface can be sketched upon and erased without damage.

Smaller, more intimate areas were created within the store — Jay Mitchell's "office," a lounge area, and a community room all serve to enrich the customer experience.

DESIGN
GRID/3 International Inc., New York, NY

STORE SIZE
223 m2 (2,400 sq. ft.)

VISUAL MERCHANDISING DESIGN
AND BRANDING
Pam Levine, Levine Design Group

FIXTURES
Existing retrofitted with LED lighting plus new from JMJ, Inc.

GENERAL CONTRACTOR
Mike Penn, Building and Remodeling Sustainable Spaces

LIGHTING
Con-Tech Lighting; Lithonia Lighting; Oggetti Luce

Bisazza Tile; Crossville, Inc. (tile); **Karastan** (carpet); **TechDesign Floors;**
Armstrong Industries (ceiling tile & vinyl base); **Sherwin Williams** (paint);
Kawneer (window frames & front door); **Cambria** (quartz slabs)

PHOTOGRAPHY
Neil Johnson

ABOVE AND BELOW: Rolex, an important product for Clarkes, is, however, exacting on how its product must be displayed and how its watch repair facilities are outfitted. The designers fulfilled the watchmaker's requirements by making the shop three feet deeper than originally planned, and entirely outfitting the watch repair area with Rolex-specified equipment. Placing the repair area in the front window proved advantageous, as the space is immaculate and customers can see that repairs are carried out on the premises.

Dell Experience Center

North Park Center, Dallas

Fitch

Columbus, Ohio

To design this prototype for Dell's first retail store, the Fitch design firm had a 230 m2 space in which to work. This Dell Experience Center's design concept features a duality that is immediately evident when the store is viewed through its mostly glass façade.

The right-hand side of the store features the signature Dell blue painted walls with a large, focal light box and the Dell logo on the back wall. On this side, and on the main dividing aisle, is shiny, white ceramic tiled flooring. Also on this side are laptop and desk-top units arranged on an under-lit, blue acrylic counter edged in metal. In the central aisle are three wood-veneered pedestals highlighting the newest and most exciting Dell products.

Three vertical glass dividers mark the entry to the left side of the store and these panels, facing the central aisle, feature lifestyle graphics and the Dell logo. These dividers are multi-purpose since they serve as vanity screens to conceal the wired portions

of the solutions stations on the left side of the store while visually branding Dell.

The left side has the same Dell blue walls but here the floors are covered with a warm-toned wood and the product display is for home theater and accessories. According to the designers, *"The flooring leads to the children's interactive area to encourage kids to experience Dell gaming products."*

The residentially arranged Home Theater Experience space, beyond the children's area, is a contemporary interpretation of what a home is like. Freestanding pedestal fixtures are covered in the same rosewood veneer as the ones on the center aisle. *"A unique aspect of the space is that all wires are concealed to show consumers a realistic view of how the product would appear in their own homes. This well thought out tenant allows the consumer to focus on the product and not be distracted by wiring systems."*

Lighting also "separates" the two areas of the store with mixed levels of light. Lighting is brighter and focused on the practical, right side but more subdued and residential on the left. The "softer" look of the Home Theater Experience also serves to entice shoppers to find out what is going on there. Where recessed cove lighting on the right adds to the ambient light, the targeted spots on the left highlight the intimate areas.

The right side of the store, with white tiled flooring, showcases the computers, while the warm-wood flooring on the left side of the store adds to the ambience of the "Home Theater Experience."

DESIGN
Fitch, Columbus, OH

STORE SIZE
230 m2 (2,472 sq. ft.)

MANAGING PARTNER, THE AMERICAS
Mike Bills

CREATIVE DIRECTOR
David Denniston

SENIOR ENVIRONMENTAL DESIGNER
Paul Teeples

GRAPHIC DESIGNER
Gabe Shultz

ACCOUNT DIRECTOR
Amy Theibert

PROJECT MANAGER
Heather Pellegrini

ARCHITECT
Fitch, inc. d/b/a Fitch, Scottsdale, AZ

GENERAL CONTRACTOR
Shrader & Martinez Construction, Sedona AZ

PHOTOGRAPHY
Mark Steele, Columbus OH

Nextel Experience Store Parque Andino

Las Condes, Santiago

In Store Diseño

Santiago

The new Nextel store shown here is located on the ground floor of the company's corporate building in Santiago's new business district.

The assignment given to Chile's In Store Diseno was to create a prototype store prior to the brand's planned re-launch in the Chilean market. What was needed was a clean, neutral and versatile retail space that would differentiate the brand from the competition and enhance consumer experience and services.

The store is fronted by a row of floor-to-ceiling windows that allows natural light to flood the space and incorporates two sets of entrance doors. Inside, these two entrances are visually connected with a

dropped, drywall ceiling panel and lighting that accentuates both entries and the products displayed between them — ensuring that neither entrance is perceived as more important than the other.

The monochromatic color scheme is interrupted only by the red furniture in the central waiting area and the red acrylic signs on the interior of the glass façade. Together, these points of bright color create a rhythm that leads the eye from one end of the store to the other.

Incorporated into the space are areas in which customers can handle products and learn about Nextel's services, with or without the assistance of sales staff. Also included, and equally important,

A semi-transparent structure houses a meeting room and the manager's office without breaking the flow of the open space.

The space includes many areas for customers to interact with the company and its products, either on their own or with the assistance of the sales staff.

DESIGN
2011, Patricio Barbosa, In Store Diseño, Santiago, Chile

STORE SIZE
248 m2 (2,669 sq. ft.)

FIXTURES / LIGHTING
Landor
In Store Diseño

PHOTOGRAPHY
Carlos Esperger

are areas where personalized customer service can take place in a relaxed, comfortable and interesting environment. The design, however, is meant to be understood as a one complete unit. Customers are allowed the freedom to explore the entire store, wondering around the various displays and information stations.

The waiting area in the center serves as a transition area between the two sides of the store; however, with easy traffic flow around the area and clear sight lines over it, the space is entirely connected.

Also maintaining the open design, and suggestive of the company's policy of transparency in customer-service, is a glass-walled, semi-transparent structure that sits mid-store and houses a meeting room and manager's office.

designer profiles

Intermezzo

Gieves & Hawkes

AMS Concept Co. Ltd.

No. 248B, Wuxing Road
Xuhui District, Shanghai, PRC
Phone: 86-21-64666296
Fax: 86-21-64455443
Email: RT@ams-cn.com, Lynn@ams-cn.com

www.ams-cn.com

Hong Kong office:
30/F, No. 8, Linze County Street
Kowloon bay, Kowloon, Hong Kong
Phone: (852)-23421151
Fax: (852)-23434708
Email: Pal@ams-hk.com

Beijing office:
Rm 308, Building 104, Qing Nian Gong
She No.3, North Chao Yang Rd
Chao Yang District, Beijing, PRC
Phone: (8610)-85790315
Fax: (8610)-85790305
Email: Jmhe@ams-cn.com

Nanning Office:
Rm.705, Unit B, Building A
Cheng Shi Bi Yuan, No.122
West Ming Xiu Rd., Nanning.
Phone/Fax: (86771)-3102036
Email: Shane@ams-cn.com

KEY PERSONNEL

Mr. Richard Tan, *Managing Director*
Email: RT@ams-cn.com

Mr. Pal Yu, *Director*
Email: Pal@ams-hk.com

Mr. Eric Xia, *Design manager*
Email: Eric@ams-cn.com

Mr. JM He, *Design manager*
Email: JM@ams-cn.com

Mr. Edward Tan, *Creative designer*
Email: Edward@ams-cn.com

Ms. Elsa Wu, *Finance manager*
Email: Elsa@ams-cn.com

Ms. Lynn Qian, *Operation manager*
Email: Lynn@ams-cn.com

Founded in 1997, AMS is a group of professionals sharing the common desire in striving for excellence in project management, architectural and interior design.

AMS is a result-orientated organization that has demonstrated the ability to get tasks done efficiently and achieving the satisfactory of all its clients. High standard and quality work is attained consistently through the compliance with ISO 9000 Quality Management guideline, which serves as an integral tool in managing everything we do.

OBJECTIVE

"To Excel Beyond Expectation" is the motto that has brought AMS to where it is today.

NETWORK

AMS comprises of multi-cultural and multi-disciplined professional team with offices covering most of Asian major cities like Singapore, Hong Kong and Kuala Lumpur, with headquarters located in Shanghai- China, where 60% of core business activities and incomes are generated.

STRENGTH

AMS-China's annual turnover can reached up to US$ 15 million with a total workforce of 300 dedicated management and staff team. The firm's major strength comes from its professional design and management team with the support of fully-owned fabrication factories in Shanghai-China, which enable AMS to provide One-Stop service to its clients from conception right up to completion of project.

FUTURE

AMS has a wide track record of projects across Mainland China, Hong Kong, Macao and other Asian countries. Presently the firm is expanding its businesses to London and other EC countries such as Italy and France. AMS is targeting EC market to account for more than 30% of its annual turnover by year 2012.

BALDAUF CATTON VON ECKARTSBERG Architects

1527 Stockton Street, 4th Floor
San Francisco, California, 94133
Phone: 415 398 6538
Fax: 415 398 6521
Email: info@bcvarch.com

www.bcvarch.com

California Academy of Sciences Retail Stores

KEY PERSONNEL
Hans Baldauf, *Principal and CFO*, baldauf@bcvarch.com
Ken Catton, *Principal and CEO*, catton@bcvarch.com
Christian von Eckartsberg, *Principal and COO*, voneck@bcvarch.com

YEAR FOUNDED
1997

NUMBER OF EMPLOYEES
25

KEY CLIENTS
Retailers: California Academy of Sciences, Taste Partners, DLew Enterprises, Cowgirl
   Creamery, Sports Basement, Oxbow Market LLC, Williams-Sonoma Inc

Restaurants: Hog Island Oyster Co, Rodrich Management Group, Il Fornaio, Gott's
   Roadside, Moana Hotel and Restaurant Group

Wineries: Franciscan Estates Winery, Cakebread Winery, Viansa Winery

Hospitality: Shangri-La Hotels & Resorts, China World Hotel

Commercial Development: Brookfield Properties Corp, The Shorenstein Company,
   Madison Marquette, The Irvine Company Retail Properties, Wilson Meany
   Sullivan, Blake Hunt Ventures, J.S. Rosenfield & Company, Ellis Partners LLP

SERVICES OFFERED
Architecture, Master Planning, Interior Design, Furnishings, Graphic Design

Baldauf Catton von Eckartsberg Architects is a San Francisco based design firm known for the diversity of scales at which it works - from the master planning of large urban projects to the tableware used in our restaurant designs. The firm's principals pursue this range of work because they believe architecture and design are richest when they are informed by the breadth and complexity of human experience. An interest in the broad approach to a design problem lends itself to the multi-disciplinary character of BCV Architects and to experiences in urban design and planning, architecture, interiors, furnishing, and graphic design.

   Baldauf Catton von Eckartsberg Architects' approach to sustainability is to examine the issue through multiple lenses – to not only seek engineering solutions but also to respond to the ethical, cultural, social, economic and historic implications of a project and its place in the environment. It is this approach that has informed projects such as San Francisco's Ferry Building Marketplace, Mercato in Bend, Oregon, the Oxbow Public Market in Napa, California and the new Master Plan for San Francisco's Treasure Island. In each of these, large conceptual ideas are refined and made meaningful by attention to the details of direct human interaction. BCV considers it essential to design projects that become vibrant communities and sustain the lives of their inhabitants and users.

SELECT AWARDS
2010
Great Places Award, American Planning Association –
   Ferry Building Marketplace
AIA|LA 6th Annual Restaurant Design Award - Bar/
   Lounge category Jury Award – *Press Club*
AIA SF Honor Award for Excellence in Interior
   Architecture – *Press Club*
Woodworks Interior Beauty of Wood Award – *Press Club*

2009
Honor Awards for Regional and Urban Design Focus on
   Mixed-Use Density – *Treasure Island Master Plan*

2008
AIA San Francisco: Special Achievement Award – *Slow
   Food Nation*
First Place Sit Down Restaurant, Retail Design Institute
   – *Anthology Supper Club*
First Place Specialty Food Shop, Retail Design Institute
   – *Press Club*

2007
EDRA/Places Design Award – *Ferry Building Marketplace*

2006
AIA San Francisco Design Award: Urban Design –
   Treasure Island Master Plan

2004
Preservation Design Award: Rehabilitation/Adaptive
   Reuse, California Preservation Foundation – *Ferry
   Building Marketplace*
Excellence in Design Award, AIA SF – *Ferry Building
   Marketplace*
Innovative Design and Construction of a New Project:
   Merit Certificate, ICSC Int'l Design & Development
   Awards – *Ferry Building Marketplace*

2003
San Francisco Architectural Heritage Award (Governor's
   Award), California Heritage Council – *Ferry Building
   Marketplace*
National Preservation Award, National Trust for Historic
   Preservation – *Ferry Building Marketplace*

2001
Best Retail Project Winner, San Francisco Business Times
   – *Olympia Place*

1999
Top Ten Great Hotel Restaurants in the World, Hotels
   Magazine – *Angelini Bangkok*

1998
International Store Interior Design, VM+SD – *Pottery Barn*

PUMA Black

Tess & Carlos

Bergmeyer Associates, Inc.

51 Sleeper Street, 6th Floor
Boston, Massachusetts, 02210-1208
Phone: 617-542-1025
Fax: 617-542-1026
Email: marketing@bergmeyer.com

www.bergmeyer.com

KEY PERSONNEL
Michael R. Davis, *Principal*
Lewis Muhlfelder, Jr., *Principal*
Joseph P. Nevin, Jr., *Principal*
David Tubridy, *Principal*

KEY CLIENTS
TD Bank, Museum of Fine Arts-Boston, West Marine, Boloco,
Lord & Taylor, Samsonite, Staples, Bassett, Cabela's, Cleveland
Museum of Art, PUMA, Talbots

NEW CLIENT CONTACT
Anne Johnson

YEAR FOUNDED
1973

SERVICES OFFERED
Architecture, Interior Design, Space Planning, Programming,
Merchandize Planning, Visual Merchandizing, Sustainable Design

Bergmeyer is a mid-sized architecture and interior design firm
that designs for a broad range of human needs and
experiences, from places where people live, work, and learn to
destinations in retail and dining. Client engagement is central
to our process. We facilitate regular conversations to get to
know what matters most on the project, so that we can design
environments that skillfully balance our clients' vision and
aesthetic preferences with practical concerns for durability,
functionality, budget, and schedule. We partner to help our
clients perfect and excel at whatever they do through strategic,
responsive, and elegant design solutions.

Collaboration is central to our process. In our office, teams
work together in rooms specifically dedicated to their client's
project and are supported by the latest technologies including
Building Information Modeling. We share the BIM model with
our consultants to enhance document quality and our in-house
LEED Coordinator works with teams to find the most
sustainable solutions for their projects resulting in LEED
Certifications at all levels, including Platinum, for many of our
clients' projects.

Foot Patrol

Brinkworth

4-6 Ellsworth Street
London E2 0AX - UK
Phone: + 44 7613 5341
Email: info@brinkworth.co.uk

www.brinkworth.co.uk

Wilson Brothers

Unit 7, 14-16 Meredith Street
London, EC1R 0AE, UK
Phone: + 44 7973 667 654
Email: info@benwilsondesign.co.uk

www.wilsonbrothers.co.uk

KEY CLIENTS
Converse, All Saints, Ben Sherman, Nike, Diesel, Karen Millen, Supreme, Heineken, Selfridges and Casio.

YEAR FOUNDED
1991

NUMBER OF EMPLOYEES
28

SERVICES OFFERED
Interior and architectural design, graphic design and art direction, digital design, communications and event marketing

Brinkworth is a design-led company working in architecture, interior design and furniture design as well as creative brand strategy and graphics. Although based in a single London office, the company has active projects all around the world.

Projects are predominantly in the areas of retail, workplace design, exhibitions, leisure and residential houses, but it is in retail — and particularly fashion retail — that Brinkworth have made their reputation. Brinkworth's most long-term retail client is fashion retailer Karen Millen, for whom Brinkworth have completed stores all over the world, designing every element from the bespoke merchandising units to all the architecture and interior design.

The company also work on exhibition projects, most recently the company designed pavilions for Converse to be installed at music festivals in the UK.

Brinkworth have designed high-end residential schemes, such as a house for shoe designer Patrick Cox, an apartment for stylist William Baker and a town house for the artist Dinos Chapman and more recently converted an 800 square meter concrete water reservoir into a weekend retreat for the artist and his family.

Brinkworth prides itself on highly creative work grounded in practical construction and business sense. The multi-disciplinary team offers a total creative process, contributing in-house design solutions at all stages from inception to completion.

Fundamental to Brinkworth's culture are collaborative partnerships, which are forged at every step of a project's development.

KEY CLIENTS
Nike, Puma, Supreme, Brooks England, Stussy, Adidas, Rapha, Honda, MTV, Twentieth Centry Fox, Sony and Virgin Atlantic.

YEAR FOUNDED
2004

SERVICES OFFERED
2D image creation and hand crafted typography, industrial design, interior and exhibition design.

The Wilson Brothers joined forces in 2004. Oscar specializes in 2D image creation and hand crafted typography, and Ben is a 3D industrial designer working with mass produced products and one off hand made commissions. Together the two accomplish highly creative projects with an international client list.

Lakeland Optical

Celia Barrett Design, LLC

3000 Old Canton Road, Suite 505
Jackson, Mississippi 39216
Phone: 601-354-0066
Fax: 601-354-9180
Email: celia@celiabarrettdesign.com

346 East 87th Street, BR
New York, New York 10128
Phone: 212-234-7545

728 Delaware Avenue
McComb, Mississippi 39648
Phone: 601-684-1689

www.celiabarrettdesign.com

KEY CLIENTS
Lakeland Optical, Hampton Inn & Suites, Holiday Inn Express, Fitness Lady Health Clubs, University Club, MCL Corp. Offices

YEAR FOUNDED
1989 New York; 1998 Mississippi

NUMBER OF EMPLOYEES
Five

AWARDS
2011 IIDA Award of Excellence, Delta Regional Chapter

2010 ASID Excellence in Design Award – Silver Retail, South Central Regional Chapter

2010 ASID Excellence in Design Award – Bronze Corporate, South Central Regional Chapter

2008 ASID Excellence in Design Award – Gold Residential, South Central Regional Chapter

2007 IIDA Award of Excellence, Delta Regional Chapter, Residential

2007 ASID Excellence in Design Award-Bronze Residential, South Central Regional Chapter

Three Sensational Spaces Awards, MS Magazine

2011, 50 Leading Business Women, MS Business Journal

Celia Barrett, A.S.I.D., I.I.D.A., is principal and owner of Celia Barrett Design, a Jackson, MS boutique interior design firm with satellite offices in New York City and McComb, MS. Ms. Barrett was a senior project designer for several leading New York City architectural firms, and a senior store designer for Macy's.

In 2011, The *Mississippi Business Journal* named Ms. Barrett as one of the "50 Leading Business Women in Mississippi" and she was awarded the Award of Excellence in Residential Design by The International Interior Design Association's Delta Regional Chapter.

Ms. Barrett is N.C.I.D.Q. certified and is the chair of the A.S.I.D. Mississippi District. She is also a member of the Better Business Bureau, the Chamber of Commerce and the US Green Building Council.

Ms. Barrett won the 2010 A.S.I.D. Silver RETAIL Excellence in Design Award for the South Central Region. She has many followers for her design blog, Designer Diner, through the website www.celiabarrettdesign.com or http://www.designerdiner. wordpress.com.

She believes that the environment in which we live and work, directly affects our ability to be productive, energized and have peace in our lives. With good communication with clients, she identifies their goals and objectives, and guides them through the design process until reaching the solution they desire.

Ms. Barrett holds a bachelor's degree in Interior Design from the Auburn University College of Architecture. She continued her studies at Auburn and Parson's School of Design in New York City in both set design and antiques. She is an adjunct professor of interior design in the department of Fine Arts at Mississippi College. She was the founder and co-artistic director, with Richard Pinter, for The Acting Group, Inc., a New York professional not-for-profit theatre company.

Celia Barrett Design is a full service design firm. Ms. Barrett and her team work with the rebranding of retail spaces and take the project from design concept to completion. The latest computer aids are used to interface with the client, larger architectural firms and contractors. With Ms. Barrett's experience at Macy's and other major firms she brings an understanding of the relationship between stores and their customers. The originality of this small firm shows in all their projects. Ms. Barrett's combined background in architectural detailing, set design and store design give her the creative advantage needed for the retail environment.

COX Communications Retail Center

Commercial Design Interiors, LLC

9121 Interline Ave, Suite 1B
Baton Rouge, Louisiana
Phone: 225-928-1190
Fax: 225-928-1199
Email: matthew@c-d-interiors.com

Licensed in Texas and Louisiana, servicing nationally

www.c-d-interiors.com

KEY PERSONNEL
Matthew Edmonds, LEED AP, ASID, IIDA
Co-Owner/Designer
Email: matthew@c-d-interiors.com

Tracy A. Burns ASID, IFMA
Co-Owner/ Designer, Woman-owned business
Email: tracy@c-d-interiors.com

KEY CLIENTS
Retail, Healthcare, Corporate, Restaurants/Bars, Sustainable

NEW CLIENT CONTACT
Matthew Edmonds

YEAR FOUNDED
2004

NUMBER OF EMPLOYEES
Five

AWARDS
2010 IIDA Awards
Award of Excellence – Hospitality, Hampton Inn & Suites
Award of Excellence – Retail, COX Communications Retail Center
Award of Excellence – Healthcare, Magnolia Assisted Living (Sustainable)
Award of Recognition – Government, Livingston Council Chambers

2010 South Central Chapter of ASID
Ovation Award Commercial– Hampton Inn & Suites
Gold Award – Hampton Inn & Suites
Silver Award – Magnolia Assisted Living (Sustainable)
Silver Award – Moto Rouge
Bronze Award – Livingston Parish Council Chambers

(Additional awards for previous years available at www.c-d-interiors.com)

Commercial Design Interiors, LLC offers commercial design experience with NCIDQ certificate holders and has registered interior designers with the State of Louisiana and Texas. The firm also has a LEED Accredited professional on staff to manage and facilitate LEED and sustainable projects.

Whether it is working, eating or shopping, the places Commercial Design Interiors, LLC creates are challenging and invigorating. The firm is less concerned with promoting a particular style and more about designing dynamic environments. Much of the work involves bringing new life to tired spaces; transforming an unproductive part of the built environment into a vibrant, integral part of the community. The firm's design process centers on a team approach to project development and delivery. Each team is responsible for a project throughout all phases of the design process. Commercial Design Interiors, LLC firmly believes the best designs result directly from dynamic collaboration between the clients and the designers.

In addition to using traditional methods of sketching, drafting and rendering, the designers make extensive use of the newest and most advanced technologies available for interior applications. This use of technology allows the firm to transfer and communicate electronic data, including drawings, to clients and consultants across the country and internationally.

Commercial Design Interiors, LLC have the experience, talent and desire to help make every client's vision of a project a reality.

Bernard Weatherill

Jones Bootmaker

Dalziel and Pow Design Consultants

5-8 Harwick Street
London, EC1R 4RG
Phone: +44 (0) 207 837 7117
Email: info@dalziel-pow.com

Also Shanghai and Mumbai

www.dalziel-pow.com

KEY PERSONNEL
David Dalziel, *Creative Director*

KEY CLIENTS
Primark, Next, John Lewis, Timberland, Topshop, Sony, Levi's

NEW CLIENT CONTACT
David Wright, *Marketing Director*

YEAR FOUNDED
1983

NUMBER OF EMPLOYEES
103

At Dalziel and Pow, they've been designing for their clients since 1983. Passionate about what they do: they create great customer experiences.

The firm develops brand environments and communications across all key touch-points and they know how to make a retail experience effective and profitable. An integrated design consultancy, Dalziel and Pow offers a full range of design services, from brand positioning, identity design and retail design, through to graphic design, photographic art direction and website design. Theirs is a holistic approach, which results in successful brand environments.

Key to the firm's success is their understanding of how customers interact with brands. Designs are developed with the customer in mind, driving brand awareness, product interaction and ultimately, sales. Over the years Dalziel and Pow have built many close working relationships with clients all over the world, including Next, Sony, Primark, Levi's, Topshop and Nokia.

Everyone at the firm takes pride in their creativity, knowledge and experience and the strength of the relationships they form with clients — key attributes of Dalziel and Pow.

RECENT AWARDS
2011
Retail Week Awards
Store Design of the Year
Topshop, Oxford Circus

2010
Drapers Awards
Best New Store or Department
Winner – John Lewis
Womenswear, Cardiff

World Retail Awards
Store Design of the Year
Winner – Topshop, New York

Retail Interiors Awards
POP Campaign of the Year
Winner – Sony

Retail Week Awards
Store Design of the Year
Winner – Primark, Bristol

ARE Design Awards USA
Specialty Store over 25,000 sq. ft.
Outstanding Merit – Topshop,
New York

Transform Awards
Best Rebrand by Sector – Retail
Silver Award – Currys

SERVICES OFFERED
Brand Definition
Brief development
Research and insights
Brand positioning
Name generation

Brand Environments
Interior design
Lighting design
Fixture design
Visual merchandising
Store planning
Shop-in-shop
Exhibition design

Brand Communications
Identity design
Navigation and signage
POS/in-store communications
Art direction
Window campaigns
Packaging design
Brand literature
Website design

Hush Puppies Kids

Guante

Rockford (RKF)

dearQ Architecture & Design

Camino el Cajon 19200 Lo Barnechea
Santiago, Chile
Phone: 56-02-8483456
Mobile: 09-8841400
Fax: 56-02-8483456
Email: marcela@dearq.cl

www.dearq.cl

dearQ Architecture & Design is an office dedicated primarily to corporate image architecture, construction and furnishing of commercial premises and offices. The firm employs architects, industrial designers, builders and graphic designers who provide comprehensive support to a wide range of clients in Chile and throughout South America. dearQ also has experience in residential and industrial architecture.

dearQ incorporates the newest materials and technology and keeps current with the latest trends in the field to ensure that its work is fresh and innovative. The firm understands the value of exceptional design to its clients and always strives for excellence in all aspects of its service.

Dalú

Evita Boutique

Privilege

Droguett A&A Ltda.

Padre Mariano 10, of. 306
Providencia, Santiago, Chile
Phone: 562 – 235 55 67
Fax: 562 – 235 17 53
Email: info@daa.cl — fd@daa.cl

www.daa.cl

KEY PERSONNEL

Freddy Droguett H. Architect, *Director*
Mauricio Muñoz Architect, *Supermarket division*
Ma. Antonieta Cepeda, *Architect, Fitness Centers and boutiques division*
Tomás González Architect, *Restaurant division*
Cristian Torres Architect, *Franchises division*
Cristian Espínola, *3D modelling and renders director*

KEY CLIENTS

Cencosud S.A., El Mundo del Vino, Sportlife, Grupo Areas, Privilege, Unifood, Nestlé, Caffarena

SERVICES OFFERED

Architecture, interior design, furniture design, lighting design

Droguett A&A was founded by Freddy Droguett H. in 1999 and is located in Santiago, the capital and largest city in Chile. From the firm's very first clients, which included El Mundo del Vino and Nestlé, to the current client roster which includes the biggest names in Chile, South America and the world, Droguett's goals have always centered on the commercial success of the finished project. The business objectives and needs of the client must be met — all else follows.

Throughout it's history Droguett and his firm have created branded spaces that faithfully represent the attributes and personality of each client's identity, and effectively communicate that identity to the end consumer — the shopper.

By using these two entities — the client and *their* client, the shopper — as sources of inspiration, the designers have been able to generate concepts and ideas that strengthen the bonds between store and consumer — between design firm and client. For many of Droguett's clients this collaboration has deepened and expanded through years of successful projects and venues. All of this produces measurable and verifiable results.

The firm naturally loves good design; however, it does not rely purely on inspiration or the blind reiteration of the newest trends. What Droguett and his team do is *listen*. They know how to hear, and empathize with, their clients, ensuring that all particulars of a project live up to, or exceed, expectations.

Everyone involved in a project participates in a systematic methodology that evaluates each element from every conceivable perspective. This systematic and team-centered strategy informs all design decisions and ensures that project management and construction proceed with speed and accuracy.

The passion that everyone at Droguett A&A brings to their work underscores their talent and expertise in uniting design and retail success.

4010 Telekom Shop

congstar

Dula (Dula-Werke Dustmann & Co. GmbH)

Harkortstraße 25-27
44225 Dortmund, Germany
Phone: +49 231 7100-0
Fax: +49 231 7100-349
Email: info@dula.de

Also Zaragoza (ESP), London (GB), Pskov (RUS), Dubai (UAE)

www.dula.de

KEY PERSONNEL

Heinz-Herbert Dustmann, *Managing Director*

KEY CLIENTS

Apple, H&M, Zara, Meyer Werft, C&A, PUMA, BMW

Presenting goods is one thing — to bring them to life in their setting quite another. It is part of Dula's concept philosophy to always regard store design in a holistic manner. This means that colors, shapes and materials, light and sound, information and presentation go hand in hand and cause an atmosphere to be created in which buying things is fun. It is with this ambition that we realize both national and international projects.

Since starting up its operations in 1953 Dula has become one of the leading European companies in the field of holistic shop design and exclusive interior fittings. 800 employees world-wide are involved in the creative planning, development, production and installation of projects that stand for individuality and rich experience value. The optical results that are possible are demonstrated by the many exemplary projects we have so far successfully realized.

Social commitment is deeply rooted in Dula's corporate culture and accompanies the entire value creating chain. Beginning with the fair treatment of all partners on the market, Dula relies upon long-term cooperative partnerships. Already during the planning process potential materials are inspected for their environmental compatibility. For example, chipboards with a low formaldehyde content and gentle powder coatings are used. We refrain from using tropic timbers to a large extent.

In the production process, health and safety at the workplace enjoys an equally high priority as does the sensitive handling of energy. Solid fuel combustion plants help to regain energy.

In its logistics system Dula uses recyclable packaging material and takes care that all materials are disposed of in a controlled fashion.

Utopia Records

Eileen Kamp

Sydney, Australia
Phone: +61 413 929 038
Email: ekamp@bigpond.net.au

Website: coming soon!

KEY CLIENTS

Westfield Limited (Australia)
Greater Union Cinemas – AHL (Australia)
Paspaley Pearls Pty Ltd (Australia)
FSW Shoes (Australia)
C Palm (Indonesia)

SERVICES OFFERED

Store Design
Visual Merchandising
Retail Design Consultation

Since 2003, Eileen Kamp has been offering Retailers and Shopping Centres the services of Store Design, Retail Design Consultation and Visual Merchandising.

With a strong understanding of how visual dynamics in retail can affect the bottom line, Eileen Kamp works one on one with her clients, both nationally and internationally, to develop tailored design solutions to create dynamic retail environments no matter how large or small the business.

STORE DESIGN:
Working through a methodical process from initial briefing through to concept development and design documentation, Eileen Kamp designs unique brand related store environments that address the specific needs and aspirations of the business and its target customers. With a selection of talented graphic designers to call upon, the stores logo and in-store signage graphics can be included in the overall design to create a cohesive image and enhance the retailers branding within the market.

While believing that even the smaller retail operators should succeed in an often tough industry, Eileen Kamp welcomes the challenge of creating practical, yet exciting stores on even the tightest of budgets.

RETAIL DESIGN CONSULTATION:
For new retailers who are finding their feet in the market, or for those established businesses who understand the importance of constant self analysis in order to stay ahead, Eileen Kamp offers one on one consultations to improve visual presentation, traffic dynamics and brand identity within the store or shopping environment.

VISUAL MERCHANDISING:
Knowing that great visual presentation of a shopping environment can inspire, educate, and entertain potential customers, Eileen Kamp and her team develop and implement unique concept installations from small window displays to large scale promotional displays for large shopping centres.

Experience has shown that good in-store merchandising can have a positive affect on the success of any retail store. Eileen and her team also assist retailers with product presentation, and traffic dynamics in order to create a motivating selling environment for sales staff and a positive shopping experience for customers.

Future Research Design Company (FRDC Pvt Ltd.)

#742, 8th A Main Cross, Off 80 feet road,
Koramangala 4th Block,
Bangalore-560034, India
Phone: 91-80-65391936
Fax: 91-80-41468424
Email: info@frdc.in

www.frdc.in

Ecko Unlimited · EKA · Crusoe

KEY PERSONNEL
Sanjay Agarwal, *Consulting and Managing Director*
Phone: +919886310645; email: sanjay@frdc.in

KEY CLIENTS
Tashi Shoes (Tata International), Ecko Unlimited (Spencer retail), Parx (Raymond), Addict (juice bar), Crusoe (mens' intimate apparel), Onida, Viveks, Nokia, ITC Ltd. (personal care division), John Players, Via (travel boutique), Eka (art store) , Max, Envy, Mr. Pretzels, Yo China, IFMPL, Fstudio (fabrics boutique), Rupee Zone (financial services), Myntra

YEAR FOUNDED
2007

NUMBER OF EMPLOYEES
24

SERVICES OFFERED
Retail Identity and concepts, Retail Design strategy, Brand Identity, Visual Merchandising, Branding, Store architectural services, Soft Experience and Service design (music, fragrance, staff attire, service brand collaterals and service wares), Green Design (LEED certified) and Roll outs so as to give a one point comprehensive solution to retailers and brand owners.

AWARDS
VMRD RETAIL DESIGN AWARDS 2009: Eka, Bangalore, India
VMRD RETAIL DESIGN AWARDS 2011:
Best Lighting Design, Tashi , Linking Store, Mumbai, India;
Best Store Front, Tashi , Linking Store, Mumbai, India

FRDC (Future Research Design Company) is a Bangalore based retail design company with exclusive licensing with internationally-reputed retail design firms ADIG Studio, San Francisco and JGA, Detroit, USA. It is a company with global vision, driven by a team of highly spirited and creative retail design professionals from India and an international team of designers and strategists. It is a consumer focused retail design company with a mission to create physical spaces which are consistent with the identity and values of the brand. It prides itself on being one of the top retail design firms in India, providing complete 360-degree retail services, including retail concepts, design strategy, retail and brand identity, visual merchandising, branding, soft experience and service design (music, fragrance, staff attire, service brand collaterals and service wares), green design (LEED certified) and roll outs, so to provide one-point comprehensive solutions to retailers and brand owners.

The Design Approach of FRDC embraces understanding the brand values, engaging the customers, putting strategy before design, story telling, bringing concept and innovation to life, combining Indian sensibilities with international visioning and showing in every project an undying passion for details. The organization is research driven. These researches are carried out by interns from major Indian and international design institutes.

The Design Process is ever evolving and yet follows certain parameters: brand therapy (involving market surveys, research, and study of client and analysis of data), concept vision (strategic as well as space vision), profile drawings, brand design extensions and concept book manual. The multidisciplinary design team lead by qualified designers and architects from premier institutes and international experience ensures that concepts created are realistic and engineerable. FRDC works with the best professionals as associates in services such as lighting design, HVAC, structure, electrical, MEP, etc., which are incorporated into, and coordinated with, the design. FRDC strives for excellence in all specifications and details and the team demands that all vendors and suppliers adhere to acceptable and approved international/national standards.

As a member of IGBC (Indian Green Building Council) and USGBC (US Green Building Council), FRDC strives to approach design from a view of sustainability. FRDC started Green Retail design two years ago with designs for Tashi (Tata International), the first LEED certified green design stores in India. The journey has picked up pace.

FRDC is powered by a team of highly motivated and extremely creative individuals who have a vision to innovate and deliver for each client. Challenging themselves and pushing the limits of observing, learning, creating, FRDC strives fearlessly for excellence; always with the aim for integrity, knowledge, passion, perfection, vision, commitment, innovation and speed in all aspects of retail design.

Judith & Charles

Key West

Brida

GHA design studios

1100 avenue des Canadiens-de-Montrèal
Bureau 130
Montréal, QC, Canada H3B 2S2
Phone: 514-843-5812 ext .229
Email: dkalisky@ghadesign.com

235 E. Main Street
Suite 107
Northville, MI 48167
Phone: 248-374-2360

www.ghadesign.com

KEY PERSONNEL
Denis Gervais, *Partner*
Steve Sutton, *Partner*
Frank Di Niro, *Partner*
Nick Giammarco, *Partner*
Paola Marques, *Partmer*
Julie Dugas, *Associate*

KEY CLIENTS:
Aéropostale, Pusateri's, H&M, Teenflo (Judith & Charles), Bravo Supermercado, Richtree

YEAR FOUNDED
1985

AWARDS
2010 Retail Store of the Year Award sponsored by Chain Store Age for Aéropostale; 2010 RDI (Retail Design Institute) for Centura Showroom; 2009 RDI for Bravo Supermercado; 2010 ICSC (International Council of Shopping Centres) U.S. Design & Development Award for Promenade in Temecula Food Court; ICSC Canadian Shopping Centre Awards for Carrefour Laval, Studio par Rona and Pickering Town Centre; 2010 SADI (Superior Achievement in Design & Imaging) for Carrefour Laval Food Court

SERVICES OFFERED
Store design, shopping centre renovations and repositioning, master retail programming, brand strategy and development

GHA is an award winning retail design firm with an international outlook culled from its unparalleled grasp of global retail. Founded in 1985, GHA has a wealth of retail experience in building memorable retail experiences. As designers for both retailers and developers, GHA has the privileged position of knowing what each one needs to succeed, what it calls "working on both sides of the lease line." With offices in Montreal and Detroit, GHA is proud of its blend of Canadian and American perspectives it brings to the international retail forum.

Clarkes Jewelers

GRID/3 International Inc.

555 Eighth Avenue, Suite 1003
New York, New York 10018
Phone: 212-391-1162
Fax: 212-273-1180
Email: design@grid3.com

www.grid3.com

KEY PERSONNEL

Ruth Mellergaard, FIIDA, *Principal*
Email: ruth@grid3.com

Keith Kovar, IIDA, FRDI, *Principal*
Email: kovar@grid3.com

YEAR FOUNDED

1980

AWARDS

2010 First Place Retail Lighting Award
for Yelton Fine Jewelry given by Con-Tech Lighting

2008 Honorable Mention Retail Lighting Award
for Robbins Diamonds given by Con-Tech Lighting

2010 Save-A-Sample award for recycling samples
for design schools

SERVICES OFFERED

Interior Design
Planning
Lighting Design
Color and Material Specification
Custom fixture details
Partnering with other professionals –
visual merchandisers, engineers, architects

GRID/3 offers design services to the retail industry with a specialty in the planning and design of jewelry stores. GRID/3 brings a hands-on approach to the creation of retail environments that attract customers and produce sales for our clients.

Planning is the unseen element that creates efficient function in a space. Planning produces the bones on which to hang the materials and brand elements of the design that set the image for the retailer. Each retail location must enhance the retailer's brand image to inform customers of the choices on offer.

Interior design takes the elements the customer sees and combines them with lighting to create an atmosphere that enforces the products on display. Lighting is not only an environmental issue but also a fiscal issue. Lighting must show a product at its best and do so while reducing overhead expenses.

GRID/3 combines all these parts into a single document that helps our clients achieve their goals and success.

Paco Rabanne

Nextel

Americanino

In Store Diseño

Domínica 367, oficina 74, Recoleta,
Santiago, Chile, 8420324
Phone: +56 2 5807400
Fax: +56 2 7320656
Email: info@instore.cl

www.instore.cl

KEY PERSONNEL
Fernando Toro Benavides (CEO)

CHIEF ARCHITECTS
Patricio Barbosa, Alicia Dulanto, Amalia Pérez,
Jaime Romero, Carolina Vásquez

KEY CLIENTS
Falabella, Nextel, Saitec, Mac Online

NUMBER OF EMPLOYEES
60

In Store Diseño is a team of young professionals dedicated to
creating, developing and implementing commercial spaces. They
are known for responding quickly to each client's requirements,
understanding that each brand is unique and has potential for
distinctive development.

Founded in 1999 by Fernando Toro, the company's experience
has positioned it as one of the leading retail design and architecture firms in Chile.

At In Store Diseño there is a clear focus on customer service,
demonstrated by the delivery of comprehensive projects that
encompasses all aspects of brand development. From the receipt
of the initial brief through every step in the process — developing
the primary image of a brand, the stages of engineering design,
supervision of construction, furniture design, visual merchandising
and finally the implementation and operation of the store — the
team at In Store Diseño is able to expertly guide clients, large and
small, in the development of a successful retail brand.

To meet the needs of its customers, the firm's team is structured
and divided into four areas of development:

- Design and implementation of shop-in-shop concepts;
- Design of department stores;
- Design and implementation of stand-alone stores;
- Production and implementation of furniture and fixtures.

While the firm's main focus has been in Chile, recent years have
seen the generation of important projects in Peru, Argentina and
Colombia. This has allowed In Store Diseño to provide continuity
and consistency to brands as they implement stores across the
region. International brands such as Mango, La Martina, Lacoste,
Benetton, Calvin Klein, Paco Rabbane, Elle, among others, rely on
In Store Diseño's regional experience.

Additionally, the team of designers and architects have been
instrumental in the design of international department store,
Falabella, as it has established a presence in Chile, Peru, Argentina
and Colombia and implemented stores ranging in size from 7,000
to 12,000 m2, two of which have LEED certification. This important
achievement has allowed In Store Diseño to develop the
knowledge and skills to design sustainable stores — becoming a
pioneer of this new and important component in the design of
retail spaces.

Mint Velvet

Jeager London

Desa

KINNERSLEY KENT DESIGN

5 Fitzroy Square,
London W1T 5HH, UK
Phone: +44 (0)20 7691 3131
Email: hello@kkd.co.uk

Office 409, Indigo Tower
Jumeirah Lakes Towers
PO Box 71645
Dubai, UAE

www.kkd.co.uk

KEY CLIENTS
ABC, Bateel, Desa, Fortnum & Mason, Historic Royal Palaces,
House of Fraser, Jaeger, London Dairy, Mercedes Benz, Mint Velvet,
Nayomi, Paris Group, P&O Ferries, Ringspun, Waitrose

NEW CLIENT CONTACT
Lindie Champion

YEAR FOUNDED
1990

NUMBER OF EMPLOYEES
25

SERVICES OFFERED
Retail Design, Retail Strategy, Branding, Graphic Design,
Interior Architecture

Kinnersley Kent Design is an independent, multidisciplinary design
consultancy specialising in retail strategy, interior and graphic design.
In short, the consultancy brings together all the elements that create
commercially successful branded environments.

Founded in 1990 by business partners Glenn Kinnersley and Mick
Kent in London, Kinnersley Kent Design today is a specialist retail
interior and graphic design consultancy with studios in London and
Dubai. Paul McElroy became a third partner in 2005.

The consultancy balances its understanding of the customer with
commercial and creative imperatives. This is where the organisation
adds value to its clients' business and rejuvenates the customer
experience.

Kinnersley Kent Design's multi-award winning work is informed by an
understanding of the commercial benefits that good design should
bring. Their strength lies in creating, evolving and repositioning retail
and leisure brands to help them perform better, whatever the demands
of the industry or environment.

AWARDS
2011
Decade of Design Competition, UAE
Presidential Commendation – Waitrose, Dubai Mall
OUTSTANDING COMMERCIAL INTERIOR DESIGN FOR RETAIL

Retail Week Awards
Highly Commended - Mint Velvet Boutique, Chichester UK
GROWING RETAILER OF THE YEAR

2010
Retail Interior Awards
Finalist - The 3 Sisters Greengrocers, Hoylake, Wirral UK
SPECIALIST STORE DESIGN OF THE YEAR

Finalist - Mint Velvet, Chichester UK
BEST SMALL SHOP DESIGN

2009
The Global Retail & Leisure International Awards
Winner - House of Fraser
UK RETAILER OF THE YEAR

Highly Commended - House of Fraser, Westfield
RLI AWARD FOR INTERIOR EXCELLENCE

Winner - Fortnum & Mason, London
RLI AWARD FOR INTERIOR EXCELLENCE

Finalist - Fortnum & Mason, London
MOST INNOVATIVE RETAIL CONCEPT OF THE YEAR

Retail Interior Awards
Winner - Destination Skin, Westfield UK
HEALTH & BEAUTY DESIGN OF THE YEAR

Winner - Waitrose Dubai Mall
FOOD & SUPERMARKET DESIGN OF THE YEAR

Retail Week Awards
Finalist - House of Fraser, Westfield London
STORE DESIGN OF THE YEAR

FX International Interior Design Awards
Finalist - Kinnersley Kent Design
INTERNATIONAL INTERIOR DESIGN PRACTICE OF THE YEAR

2008
Retail Interiors Awards
Winner - Fortnum & Mason, Piccadilly
SHOPFITTING EXCELLENCE AWARDS

Finalist -House of Fraser, Victoria Square, Belfast
DEPARTMENT STORE INTERIOR OF THE YEAR

Yusty
Arenal2

Euro-optica
OhmyGOd

marketing azz®

Huelva 16, Bloque 2
Estudio 54
28100 Alcobendas
Madrid, Spain
Phone: +34 91 484 02 30
Email: info@marketing-jazz.com

www.marketing-jazz.com

KEY PERSONNEL
Carlos Aires, *Founder & Principal*

KEY CLIENTS
Pharmacy: Loreal, Farmacia Arenal, Farmacia Santa Maria, Farmacia Santa Cruz. *Optics:* Luxottica, Euro-optica y Eurosone, Sonooptica. *Beauty Care:* Sephora España, Procter & Gamble Salon Professionals. *Wine:* Marques de Riscal. *Fashion*: Yusty. *Luxury:* OhmyGOd. *Restaurants:* Patatin & Patatan. *Entertainment:* Walt Disney España

NEW CLIENT CONTACT
Carlos Aires
Email: carlos@marketing-jazz.com

YEAR FOUNDED
2002

NUMBER OF EMPLOYEES
Seven

SERVICES OFFERED
Cool Store Design + Branding and Windows presentation + Visual Merchandising Training Programs

Madrid-based firm MARKETING-JAZZ specializes in *visual marketing* — with an emphasis on the "visual" half of that phrase. Founder and principal Carlos Aires insists that the "seeing" and the "selling" cannot be separated. He and his team involve themselves in every element within the shopper's line of sight. Every display case, sign, logo, window and printed communication — in addition to the overall design of the space — are all designed to contribute to the clarity of the brand message.

Defining this brand message is the first step for any project undertaken by the firm. Generating this single, powerful idea — this distinguishing feature — must happen first, all else follows. Not that the "all else" is easy. Every aspect of the design that follows must contribute to the communication of the brand message to anyone entering or even walking by the store.

MARKETING-JAZZ was founded in 2003 when Aires was given the opportunity to design window displays for Yusty, a menswear retailer in Madrid. Over the following years the window displays that Aires designed for Yusty grew into a complete marketing message that included store design, advertising and even direct mail. Right from the start Aires understood the importance of connecting and unifying the many visual messages radiating from a retailer.

The firm also strongly believes that the relationship with the client doesn't end the day the store opens. The designers stick around to see how the store works: touching up aspects of the design, changing the products promoted in the windows and training the staff to better merchandise the environment. This training is not an afterthought for MARKETING-JAZZ but a vital component of its business. In addition to the assistance given to each client, the firm is involved in various visual merchandising training programs throughout Spain.

The marketing aspects of the firm's name, MARKETING-JAZZ, are clear, but what about the jazz? Music is not only incorporated into the name of the firm, it also runs as a metaphor through Aires' design and marketing philosophy. The defining qualities of jazz — innovative, flexible, free-spirited, creative, in-the moment, exciting — could also be used to describe the approach MARKETING-JAZZ takes toward its work. Much like a great jazz ensemble, Aires and his team design to the needs of each situation, instantly reacting to new directions and challenges.

Kidrobot

9026 Eyes

MASHstudios Inc.

12705 Venice Blvd
Los Angeles, California 90066
Phone: 310-313-4700
Fax: 310-313-6800
Email: info@mashstudios.com

www.mashstudios.com

KEY PERSONNEL

Bernard Brucha, *Principal*
bernard@mashstudios.com

KEY CLIENTS

Kidrobot,7 For All Mankind, Steven Alan, Alexis Bitar,
Microsoft, The Limited, 9026 Eyes

NEW CLIENT CONTACT

Bernard Brucha

YEAR FOUNDED

2002

NUMBER OF EMPLOYEES

10

SERVICES OFFERED

Retail Design, Millwork Fabrication, Office Interiors,
Branding

MASHstudios is a multidisciplinary Los Angeles based design firm that combines award winning design and engineering experience with local manufacturing capabilities, all with the goal of creating timeless design.

Founded in 2002 by Bernard Brucha, MASHstudios is supported by a diverse team of designers, architects and engineers grounded in the core competencies of industrial design and fabrication.

The cornerstone of MASHstudios' philosophy is client-centered service. The design firm includes clients in every step of the process, and is dedicated to providing as much attention to the finest details as it does to the big picture. MASHstudios promises competency, dedication and innovation from each member of its team.

Through consistent use of modern forms and responsible materials, MASHstudios ensures longevity and durability in all of its designs. Superior engineering skills support the firm's standard of producing only high-quality, built-to-last products. MASHstudios' local manufacturing capabilities allow it to have control over every step of the process, while also minimizing its carbon footprint.

Worth Avenue News

PDT International

2495 East Commercial Blvd
Fort Lauderdale, Florida 33308
Phone: 954-533-7240
Fax: 954-616-8434
Email: info@pdtintl.com

www.pdtintl.com

KEY PERSONNEL

Sven Pavlik, *Partner,* sven@pdtintl.com
Luis Martin, *Partner,* lmartin@pdtintl.com

NUMBER OF EMPLOYEES

35

SERVICES OFFERED

Planning, Design, Project Implementation, Graphic Design

PDT International is a full service design firm, providing innovative ideas and design strategies to leading corporations around the world.

The firm's specialty lies in the customer "experience" and using that experience to develop market-driven designs maximized for performance and profitability. As a company, PDT International is committed to redefining the way people live, play, work, and shop. PDT International's strengths go far beyond pure design solutions; it is the firm's ability to create strategies that serve specific objectives that set it apart from the rest. PDT International's award-winning design team has developed successful Brand Strategies, Flagship Stores, Prototypical Retail Stores, Design Enhancements, Shop Concepts, Store-Within-A-Store and Category Management Programs for many clients since its inception.

PHILOSOPHY

PDT International's brand starts with passion; the firm is unified under the same vision and values. PDT International stands for: creativity in all it does, global in its culture and demographics, innovative in its approach, unique, spirited and bold. The team is a consumer focused group that works in collaboration to create solutions that get results and add value to the team, the consumer, the client and the industry.

APPROACH

Initially, PDT International's strategic assessment involves information gathering for it to develop a depth of understanding of where a client is today, and its future goals. The next task includes determining and verifying the key sensory elements and the emotion of the client's business, which will enable PDT International to determine the "feel". Using information learned from the assessment, goals and emotions, PDT International develops a design concept which provides the framework for further client collaboration and "Team" interaction that refines this concept to a final design. This final concept is then transformed by PDT International's production team into workable details and drawings for project implementation.

PDT International's approach is holistic – from the first forecasting and planning exercise to the creation of a new prototype — the firm is deeply involved in all components of each project. As specialist in brand creation, interpretation and implementation, PDT International captures and articulates its clients' needs today and in the future and creates the tools that are necessary to consistently embody that at every point of customer contact.

PUMA

Levi's Icon Store "Buttenheim"

plajer & franz studio

Erkelenzdamm 59-61
10999 Berlin, Germany
Phone: +49 30 616 558 0
Email: studio@plajer-franz.de

www.plajer-franz.de

KEY PERSONNEL

Alexander Plajer, *Principal*
Werner Franz, *Principal*

NUMBER OF EMPLOYEES

45

KEY CLIENTS

BMW Group, PUMA, Timberland Europe, s.Oliver, Samsung, Galeries Lafayette, Adessa, Estée Lauder, Salewa

SERVICES OFFERED

Architecture, Interior Architecture, Consultancy, Conceptual Design, Design and Planning, Graphic Design

The company founders, architects alexander plajer & werner franz, gained their initial international experience in New York at the office of Richard Meier and Tsao & McKown. Here they both spent several years working with clients in the United States and the middle and far east before moving back to Germany to set up their own company in Berlin in 1996. In over a decade of creative and imaginative partnership, they built up an impressively broad-ranging portfolio with an international client base. Today plajer & franz studio with their team of 45 employees has an international reputation for innovative excellence and a superb sense of style. Their projects are regularly featured in publications worldwide.

The development of brand architecture and corporate identity in retail as well as the design of premium hotels and resorts form the core of the firm's expertise. plajer & franz studio has an international reputation for innovative excellence,

quality down to the smallest detail, great planning skills and a superb sense of style.

From private yacht to automobile trade stands via award-winning bars and luxury hotels, the key to plajer & franz studio's freshness of vision lies in their continuous exploration and cross-fertilisation between disciplines and areas of experience. The firm's ability to deliver show-stoppingly innovative design with elegant and meticulous finishing and precise details lies with its ability to take what they learn in one area and applying it, where appropriate, in another: high tech material forming from the car industry, for example, may yield exciting new surfaces for a shop-in-shop project, whereas new developments in the use of digital display techniques from the bar and club scene might fit perfectly with a new automobile display concept – it 's all in the mix!

At plajer & franz studio all project stages, from concept to design as well as roll-out supervision, are carried out in-house by plajer & franz' hand-picked team of 45 architects, interior and graphic designers. Special project-based groups work on overall interior and building construction projects and on communication and graphic design. plajer & franz studio have also established themselves in the premium sector of luxury residential projects and hotels in both Europe and Asia; these include a recently completed hotel in Porto, a five star resort in Croatia and 50,000 m2 premium serviced apartments on the Portuguese coast.

Plus Construction Group

Prol. Av. De los bosques 1506 piso 2 c.p.52780
Tecamachalco, Estado de México
Phone: 52451096 – 52451291 - 52451589
Fax: 52451589 Ext.237
Email: t.plusart@gmail.com

www.cplus.com.mx

NEW CLIENT CONTACT
Lic. Tadeo Carreño Cole, email: t.plusart@gmail.com

AWARDS
International Design Awards, Honorable Mention, Vespa

Over the course of its 45-year history, Plus Construction Group has successfully designed and built a multitude of industrial, commercial and residential projects. Clients such as Modelo Brewery, the music-store chain Mix-up and entertainment companies iShop and Apple have all benefited from the firm's high standards in customer service, quality of design, workmanship, and professionalism.

Plus Construction Group's experienced team of architects and engineers are always available and willing to face new challenges and partner with their clients to produce the best possible results for each project. As they reinvent and redefine the aesthetic principles of design – pushing the boundaries and taking risks when needed or respecting conservative standards when appropriate — each employee contributes to the firm's continued development both in Mexico and internationally.

Riis Retail A/S

Gejlhavegaard 31
Denmark 6000, Kolding
Phone: 70243100
Email: Mail@riis-retail.com

www.riis-retail.com

KEY PERSONNEL

Dennis Madsen, *Creative Director*
Email: dam@riis-retail.com

KEY CLIENTS

Bestseller, Skoringen, 3 (cellphone operator), Jack & Jones, Selected, Only, Vero Moda

SERVICES OFFERED

Design, 3d visualization, manufacturing, worldwide sourcing, construction,
maintenance and after sale.

Riis Retail supplies successful retail solutions to more than 500 stores worldwide — each year.
The firm works in 45 countries and has a broad experience from a wide variety of industries. The
goal at Riis Retail is to create solutions that extend its clients' business potential and enhance
their overall brand perception.

Riis Retail delivers complete retail solutions for some of the world's most popular brands. It
develops and manufacture store concepts and takes care of everything — from the first line
drawing and construction work to the purchase, fitting and maintenance of the store.

The firm calls the phases Design, Build, Source and Maintain, and instills the entire process
with its passion for original ideas, its craft skills and its business acumen.

A key element of successful retailing is the creation of retail spaces that tell stories and offer
customers authentic experiences. All new retail concepts are created in the interplay between a
vast knowledge of materials and a keen eye for detail. The experienced design team at Riis Retail
is among the best in the industry and each shop they design is guaranteed to be at the very
forefront of retailing and a trendsetter in its sector.

Riis Retail has the capability to deliver complete retail solution that help to lift its clients'
brand to new commercial heights.

COX Communications Retail Center

Ritter Maher Architects, LLC

4880 Bluebonnet Blvd.
Baton Rouge, Louisiana
Phone: 225-383-4321
Fax: 225-383-4323
Email: info@rittermaher.com

www.rittermaher.com

KEY PERSONNEL
Scott Ritter, *Principal*
Email: sritter@rittermaher.com

Steve Maher, *Principal*
Email: smaher@rittermaher.com

Amy Comeaux, Intern Architect

NEW CLIENT CONTACT
Scott Ritter

YEAR FOUNDED
2003

NUMBER OF EMPLOYEES
Eight

Ritter Maher Architects is an energetic and progressive firm
that is involved in projects across the southeast. RMA has an
established track record of successful projects and was recently
named one of the top 10 largest firms in the greater Baton
Rouge area. RMA has a wide variety of project expertise and
can offer clients a full range of services.

holpe+

rkd retail/iQ

gpf witthayu towers suite 703-704 tower A
93/1 wireless road
bangkok 10330 thailand
Phone: +66225531550
Email: talk2us@rkdretailiq.com

shanghai / shenzhen / hong kong / mumbai / dubai

www.rkdretailiq.com

KEY PERSONNEL

RKurt Durrant, *president & idea man*
email: rkurt@rkdretailiq.com

KEY CLIENTS

DFS Galleria, China Resources, Suning, Parkson

NEW CLIENT CONTACT

RKurt Durrant

YEAR FOUNDED

1987

NUMBER OF EMPLOYEES

50+

AWARDS

To date 11 projects have been recognized by a variety of
leading international retail industry organizations yielding
22 awards for retail planning and design excellence.

rkd retail/iQ is full service retail design consultancy specialized in
delivering complete branded retail environments across all retail
formats and channels.

Retail planning + design / retail + environmental graphics / retail
architecture / retail strategy.

Through its convergent process of retail strategy and retail
planning + design, rkd retail/iQ partners with clients who share a
common vision of positioning their retail brand in the competitive
world market.

Celebrating 24 years of specific Asian retail planning and design
experience in 2011, rkd retail/iQ has completed hundreds of retail
projects with dozens of clients resulting in millions of square meters
of implemented retail and multiple awards.

rkd retail/iQ has directed/participated/completed retail projects in
20 countries and developed programs that have been implemented
in a further 15 countries.

Through organic expansion rkd retail/iQ has evolved into 6 group
offices in China (Shanghai, Shenzhen, Hong Kong), India (Mumbai),
MENA (Dubai) with the group head quarters in Thailand (Bangkok).
rkd retail/iQ currently staffed by 50+ retail design team members
from an exciting and diverse variety of experiences and cultures.

Verona Vibe

Ruscio Studio

2197 Sherbrooke E.
Montréal, Québec, Canada H2K 1C8
Phone: 514-276-0600
Fax: 514-276-6604
Email: info@rusciostudio.com

www.rusciostudio.com

KEY CLIENTS
Starbucks
American Apparel
National Bank of Canada
Linen Chest
Souris Mini
Mark's

AWARDS
Floor Focus 2011 Vision Awards
Retail category winner
Project: Magico Imperial

Chain Store Age Awards 2010
Honorable Mention - Soft Line Category
Project: Verona Vibe

A.R.E. Design Awards 2010
Fixture of the Year
Project: Mark's Walk-in Freezer Lab

VMSD 2010 Retail Renovation Competition
Renovation of the Year
Project: Underground

GIA World 2010
Global Innovator Award
Project: Stark & Whyte

SERVICES OFFERED
Concept development
Brand development
Project management
Mall renovation / expansion
Tenant reviews
Site surveys
Site supervision & coordination
Permit expediting

ROBERT RUSCIO BIOGRAPHY
President/Principal Designer
President and Principal Designer of Ruscio Studio, Robert Ruscio is a 25 year veteran in the retail design industry and is widely recognized in the field for his passion and talent in the conceptualization of retail spaces.

Having gained valuable experience in various commercial design firms where he worked as team leader on "roll-out" projects such as Timberland, Aldo, Pegabo, Les Ailes de la Mode, San Francisco, Dynamite, Stokes, etc., Robert stepped out on his own and created Ruscio Studio in 2002.

RUSCIO STUDIO
Now in its 10th year, Ruscio Studio has grown into an interior retail design firm that is recognized, both nationally and internationally, by retailers and malls alike.

With a reputation for a current and fresh approach to retail concepts, it is the fusion of design expertise with wide retail knowledge that makes Ruscio Studio uniquely specialized. The firm listens to its clients and offers them complete expertise to fulfill their needs, yet never loses sight of the main purpose of its involvement — RETAIL.

Ruscio Studio is driven by the pride of its work and the ability to "turn on a dime". Understanding deadlines and being challenged is what the firm has come to expect. The team holds over 100 years of combined experience directly in the field and is ready to deliver to its clients.

Ruscio Studio has been honored with over 70 local and international awards from respected organizations such as ARE, ICSC, VMSD and SADI.